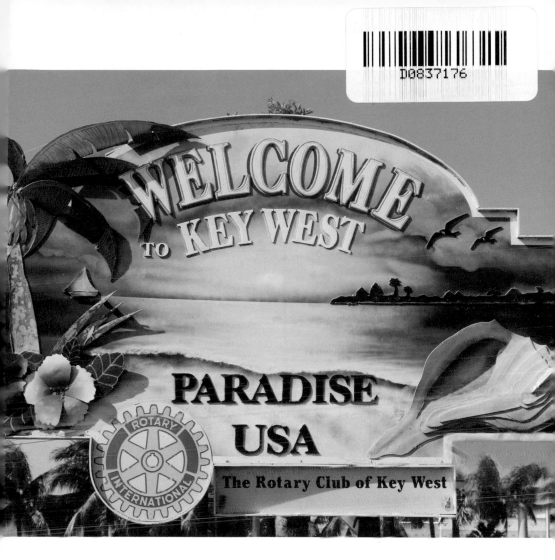

KEY WEST IN HISTORY

A GUIDE

TO MORE THAN 50 SITES IN
HISTORICAL CONTEXT

RODNEY AND LORETTA CARLISLE

PINEAPPLE PRESS   Sarasota, Florida

Inquiries should be addressed to:
Pineapple Press, Inc.
P.O. Box 3889
Sarasota, Florida 34230
www.pineapplepress.com

Library of Congress Cataloging in Publication Data
Carlisle, Rodney P.
 Key West in history / Rodney and Loretta Carlisle.
      pages cm
 Includes bibliographical references.
 ISBN 978-1-56164-796-5 (pbk. : alk. paper)
 1. Key West (Fla.)--History. I. Carlisle, Loretta. II. Title.
 F319.K4C35 2015
 975.9'41--dc23
                                2015021733

Design by Doris Halle
Printed in the USA

Contents

Contents

Contents

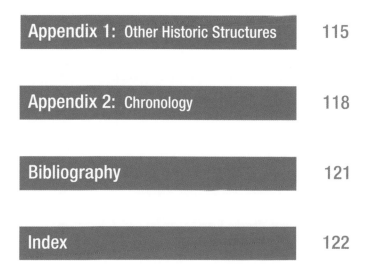

This map shows some of the often visited sites, as well as some that are off the beaten path. The book also covers 35 more sites, with addresses listed in the text.

Key West

1 Key West Lighthouse
Truman and Whitehead (SW side)

2 Basilica of St. Mary, Star of the Sea
Truman Ave. and Windsor Lane

3 Bahama Village
Corner of Duval and Petronia Streets

4 Sculpture Garden/Wrecker Monument
Wall and Tift Streets (N side Wall)

5 Oldest House (322 Duval)
W side of Duval between Eaton and Caroline

6 Fort Zachary Taylor
On point at foot of Southard Street

7 East Martello Tower
S. Roosevelt Blvd. between two branches of Feraldo Court

8 West Martello Tower
Beach side of White Street and Atlantic Blvd.

9 African Cemetery
Higgs Beach just E of West Martello Tower, at White Street and Atlantic Blvd.

10 Gatoville Pocket Park
1/2 block E of Simonton Street, on S side of Louisa

11 José Martí Monument
Corner Virginia and José Martí Streets, in corner of park

12 *Maine* Memorial
At the corner where Passover Lane joins Margaret Street, in the cemetery

13 Flagler Station
NE corner of Margaret and Caroline Streets

14 Coast Guard Cutter *Ingham*
Moored at foot of Southard Street, just N of entrance to Ft. Zachary Taylor Park

15 Truman White House
Entrance from Caroline and Front Streets

16 HAWK Missile Radar Tower
End of Government Road (off Flagler) just N of Key West Airport

17 AIDS Memorial
Beach side of corner White Street and Atlantic Blvd.

Introduction

In recent decades, Key West, Florida, has flourished as a tourist destination. More than a million visitors arrive annually by cruise ship, airplane, ferry, tour bus, and automobile. The modern attractions of the small city reflect its rich history. The overlay of commercial attractions, unique architecture, free spirit, and historic sites make the city a one-of-a-kind location. With its continuing heritage as an art colony that colorfully combines Bahamian, Cuban, and Caribbean cultural strains, and set in a subtropical climate, Key West has a unique charm.

Because of its locale, Key West has played crucial roles in history. Like some other cities in the United States, "local history" is much more than just a story of a few town founders or nearby battles, because the place repeatedly played a prominent role in national and international events through war and peace, boom and bust, relapse and recovery.

Our focus in this book is not just local history, but instead, how the people, events, and places of Key West played into larger history. We have organized the book by periods, showing how various landmarks, buildings, museums, and commercial attractions reflect *Key West in History*. We start with the early settlement of Key West by pioneers who first got title to the land, and with the story of the first U.S. naval outpost in the town.

Following chapters cover:
- the wrecker era, when local ship captains and their hardy crews made a business out of salvage from wrecked sailing vessels;

- the Civil War era, when the city played a crucial role as a Union outpost in the Confederate South;
- the age of enterprise, when new businesses came to Key West;
- the era of "Cuba Libre," when Cuban patriots and the Cuban War of Independence dominated life in the town;
- the early twentieth century, when Key West became a haven for artists and writers;
- World War II, when the city's strategic location was again crucial to the defense of the United States;
- the recent decades of rebirth as a tourist destination.

For local historians, the structures, artifacts, memorials, and mementos carefully collected as part of local heritage all represent multi-dimensional documentation of the past. These objects and places often tell more than a preserved manuscript or old book. A pile of coins from a sunken treasure ship, a moss-gray gravestone, the weathered walls of an old fort, or the elegant mansion of a once proud merchant from a past century— all tell stories. Sites and artifacts serve as pathways to the past for the public, both local residents and visitors. So this book focuses on places, buildings, collections, and artifacts that you can visit to learn more about the role of the city in history.

For each period, we briefly review Key West's role in broader events and trends, then focus on a selection of more than fifty easily visited sites around the city that physically reveal aspects of the developments. An appendix lists other sites rich in historical value. Most are private, viewable only from the outside. A second appendix is a chronology, showing the place of Key West in history. A bibliography lists some of the major print and Internet sources that we recommend if you want to delve a bit deeper into Key West history.

*Top: **John W. Simonton** (1789–1854) pioneered Key West by purchasing the island of Cayo Hueso from Juan Pablo Salas for $2,000 on January 19, 1822. His bust is one of many in the Key West Sculpture Garden, just off Mallory Square.*

*Bottom: **Harry S. Truman**, President of the United States from 1945 to 1953, wintered in Key West in the navy base commandant's housing beginning in 1946. The "Little White House" where he stayed is one of the city's major historical attractions.*

1 Perilous Waters

Everyone, it seems, has heard of the Spanish explorer Ponce de León and his legendary search for the Fountain of Youth. Ponce's first landing was somewhere a few miles south of present-day St. Augustine on April 2, 1513. He named the new land *Pascua de Florida,* or "Spring Passover," for the date of his discovery, then sailed south along the Florida Atlantic Coast. On that voyage, he discovered the Bahama Channel before sailing west through the Florida Straits, the passageway between the Florida Keys and Cuba.

Thus it was Ponce de León who discovered the route around the southern tip of Florida that would become the major sea highway for Spanish treasure ships and, later, for modern cargo carriers, passenger liners, cruise ships, fishing boats, and private yachts. As we will detail, the waterway would later see privateers and pirates, blockade-runners and naval patrols, smugglers and wreck-salvors, submarines and destroyers. The waters proved treacherous, especially during storms. Even so, the Gulf Stream flowing through the Florida Straits aids mariners sailing from the Gulf of Mexico out into the Atlantic, carrying ships along eastward and northward in the 5- or 6-knot current that runs past the coast of Florida.

On his trip through the straits, Ponce de León discovered the Florida Keys and named them the "Martyrs." According to the narrative of Antonio de Herrera, who chronicled Ponce's trip: "To all this line of islands and rock islets they gave the name of The Martyrs because, seen from a distance, the rocks as they rose to view appeared like men who were suffering; and the name remained fitting because of the many that have been lost there since." Thousands of lives lost to storms would prove Antonio de Herrera right about the fitting nature of Ponce's name for the Keys.

After passing by Key West, Ponce made his way up the Gulf Coast of Florida to somewhere near present-day Pensacola. Before returning to Puerto Rico, he spotted the Dry Tortugas, naming them for the nesting turtles he saw there. According to one story, the term "Dry Tortugas" is an English corruption of *Tres Tortugas,* or "Three Turtles," with the English name later adopted because mariners found the islands devoid of fresh water.

Ponce de León got a grant from Spain to govern the lands he had discovered. However, when he returned in 1521 to make a settlement near present-day Sanibel Island, he and his men were attacked by Calusa Indians, known and feared by other Florida natives as effective warriors. Ponce suffered a wound from an arrow in the attack and abandoned the settlement. He died in July 1521 from an infection of the wound.

Florida remained part of the Spanish Empire from the time of Ponce's discovery until 1763, when it was taken by the British. After the American War of Independence (1775–1781), Florida returned to Spanish control from 1783 until Spain ceded the territory to the United States in 1821. In that exchange the United States agreed to pay up to $5 million in

Cayo Hueso or "Bone Key" was the original Spanish name for Key West. This sign in the shape of a cigar band is found on the east side of the Wall Warehouse at Mallory Square, which now houses the restaurant El Meson de Pepe and a museum devoted to Key West's Cuban heritage.

outstanding claims against Spain arising from Florida cases. The U.S. got Florida's 42 million acres at less than 12 cents an acre. It was a bargain.

Cayo Hueso and Key West

The British practice of corrupting names of places from other languages into something more easily pronounced by English-speakers is the generally accepted explanation for the name "Key West." In Spanish, the island was originally known as *Cayo Hueso,* or Bone Key, apparently for the heaps of fish bones left there by camping Native Americans. *Cayo Hueso* was easier for English speakers to say as "Key West." The name stuck because Key West is the most westerly of the keys that lie like stones on a giant necklace from the eastern tip of Florida almost due west in a line for more than 100 miles.

The seas between Cuba and Key West could be extremely hazardous. In the age before steamships, ships propelled by wind power and sails often wrecked on the rocks and sandbars when driven by winds from the south. In the Spanish and British periods, before settlement by the Americans, hundreds of ships wrecked among the nearby shoals and islands, where pirates often watched for ships in distress or cargo ships unaccompanied by armed

Key West "Conchs"

Even before the United States acquired Florida from Spain, Bahamians visited the Florida Keys to cut timber, salvage wrecked ships, and sometimes fish and catch turtles. So even before American settlement, some Bahamians stayed in the keys, although there is no record they made any permanent settlement.

When wealthy British loyalists fled from the United States to the Bahamas after the American Revolution, they disparagingly called the local residents of the Bahamas "conchs" because they were known for eating the shellfish. When Bahamians settled in Key West through the 1800s, they called themselves conchs and were called that by others. A great many of the early permanent residents of the Florida Keys could trace their ancestry to Bahamian settlers, and it became a point of pride to call themselves conchs.

In the twentieth century, older residents of Key West (no matter their ancestry) began to call themselves conchs to distinguish themselves from newcomers and visitors. In recent decades there has been a refinement: residents who have lived in Key West for more than seven years have earned the right to call themselves "Saltwater Conchs"; residents for less than seven years are "Freshwater Conchs."

These Spanish pieces of eight were recovered from the wreck of the *Atocha*, the greatest sunken treasure recovered in modern times.

escorts. Between the hazards of storms and pirates, the dangerous reputation continued well into the period of American control.

First Settlement

Although Key West remained in nominal Spanish control for three centuries (except for the brief twenty-year British interlude from 1763 to 1783), neither Spain nor Britain set up any permanent settlements there. Pirates and Bahamian turtle fishermen were known to make only transient camps, as had some groups of Native Americans before them. So when American settlers arrived in 1821, they were the first residents of Key West who intended to stay, and the first to try to impose any system of law and order. That turned out to be a challenge.

American settlers brought their opportunistic and entrepreneurial spirit to Key West. Some would see the possibilities in land values, others saw the strategic location, and some saw the salvage of ships and cargoes as a profitable business, finding ways to produce a profit from the unique climate and setting. The heritage began to form.

Unlike most other parts of the American frontier of the early decades of the republic, all settlers to Key West had to come by sea. So they brought their memories of seaports from New England, the Middle Atlantic, and the coastal Southern states, as well as from Cuba and the Bahamas, to the little community. Throughout Key West, churches, museums, and the lighthouse itself document the hazards of the dangerous waters, while the town's residential and commercial structures attest to the blend of cultural heritages.

SITES

MEL FISHER MUSEUM AND THE *ATOCHA*
200 Greene Street

As early as 1566, the Spanish began sending annual treasure fleets from their holdings in the New World to Spain, consisting of galleons in well-armed fleets or armadas. One of the armada routes ran from Cartagena in present-day Colombia and Portobello in present-day Panama to Havana, Cuba, where they would rendezvous with another fleet from Veracruz in Mexico. The 1622 voyage of the treasure

ship *Neustra Señora de Atocha* ("Our Lady of Atocha"—named for a church in Madrid) was delayed by loading the immense treasure that had been packed over the Isthmus of Panama for shipment from Portobello. Eventually a 28-ship convoy of galleons and auxiliary vessels sailed for Spain from Havana on September 4, 1622. Even then mariners knew very well that the storm season for the Caribbean and the Gulf of Mexico begins in mid- or late August and continues into the fall months, but the fleet sailed anyway.

Two days and about 50 miles out of Havana, off the Dry Tortugas, the 1622 armada was struck by a hurricane, driving the *Atocha* and a sister ship, the *Santa Margarita,* onto coral

At 200 Greene Street, the Mel Fisher Maritime Museum contains treasures from the *Atocha,* as well as historic displays of other shipwrecks and materials on piracy and the slave trade. It also offers lab tours demonstrating historical conservation methods.

These shackles on display at the Mel Fisher Maritime Museum were used aboard the slave ship *Henrietta Marie.* The small size of some of the shackles shows that even children were kept in such ankle restraints aboard slave ships. Often two slaves would be shackled together with a single bilbo.

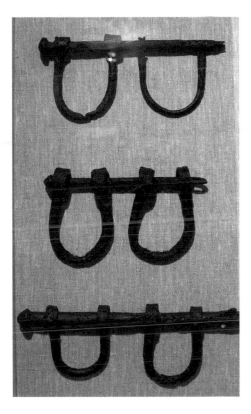

reefs. The ships sank in relatively shallow waters, with the *Atocha* going down some 55 feet. The Spanish never located the exact spot of the loss of *Atocha,* but spent ten years salvaging about half of the cargo of the *Santa Margarita.* With the equipment available at the time, salvage was difficult, made harder by further storms scattering wreckage and cargoes. The Spanish used a primitive diving bell, but the workers, mostly slaves, often died from decompression or drowning.

The recorded treasure of the *Atocha* was immense, with the major cargo made up of 24 tons of silver bullion in 1,038 ingots. In addition there were some 52 chests of silver coins, 582 copper ingots, and 125 gold bars and discs. Other cargo included indigo, tobacco, 1,200 pounds of worked silverware, and large amounts of unregistered jewelry smuggled aboard to avoid taxes.

Dive shop entrepreneur Mel Fisher moved from California to Florida to search for sunken treasure, and in 1969 he began a sixteen-year quest to locate the treasure of the *Atocha.* The search was spurred on when bits of the scattered cargo were located in 1973, including some silver bars with the correct stamp. A larger partial payday of some $20 million came in 1980 when the Fisher crew recovered a cargo of gold bars from the wreck of the *Santa Margarita.* In 1985, the Fisher team made an even more dramatic find, the main cargo of the *Atocha,* yielding an immense fortune in silver bars, pesos, and jewelry. After a strenuous court fight against claims by the State of Florida for the treasure, Fisher succeeded in retaining the bulk of the $450 million, one of the largest lost treasures ever recovered.

In 1987 Fisher bought a building that had once served as the Key West Naval Station headquarters to house the Mel Fisher Maritime Museum. Visitors today learn the story of the *Atocha* and other treasure ships, view some of the silver bars and piles of silver pesos recovered from the wreck, and learn more about other archaeological finds.

LIGHTHOUSE AND LIGHTHOUSE KEEPER'S QUARTERS

As soon as the United States took over Florida and Key West, one of the first orders of business for the U.S. government was to set up navigation aids to help reduce the threat of shipwreck in the perilous waters off Key West and around the

Climbing the 88 steps to the top of the Key West Lighthouse provides visitors with a spectacular view of the town, harbor, and surrounding islands.

state. Lt. Matthew Perry, in command of the U.S. naval schooner *Shark,* wrote to the secretary of the navy:

> The great number of vessels that daily pass through the Gulf of Florida, to and from Ports of Cuba, Jamaica and the Spanish Main renders the erection of Light Houses, not only as an act of justice on the part of our Government, But humanity and a regard to the safety of the lives and fortunes of our citizens seriously demand so desirable a measure.

Perry recommended the installation of lights in the Keys and one in the Dry Tortugas. Over the period 1825–1827, the government authorized four lighthouses, including one in Key West and one on Garden Key in the Dry Tortugas; additionally, a lightship was anchored on Carysfort Reef near Key Largo in the same period.

Perry surveyed the island and harbor in 1822, claiming the island for the United States. Perry renamed Key West as Thompson Island, after the then Secretary of the Navy Smith Thompson. The name never stuck.

Displays at the Lighthouse Keeper's Quarters tell the story of the Key West Lighthouse and the lighthouse keepers who maintained it. Michael and Barbara Mabrity were the first keepers, and this building, erected in 1887, was the home of Mabrity descendants who maintained the light well into the twentieth century.

The story of the Key West lighthouse recommended by Perry is commemorated in the Lighthouse Museum at 938 Whitehead Street. The first lighthouse in the city was built in 1825 on Whitehead spit. Michael Mabrity, from St. Augustine, was appointed the first lighthouse keeper. The lighthouse tower itself was built of brick and stood 47 feet from the ground to the base of the lantern. On Mabrity's death in 1832, his wife, Barbara, took over the job. She was one of only a few women lightkeepers in the era.

In 1864, during the Civil War, the aging Barbara Mabrity was suspected of pro-Confederate leanings and was fired. The duties were taken over by John J. Carroll, husband of one of Barbara's granddaughters. When he passed away, the job passed to the husband of another granddaughter of Barbara Mabrity. Altogether, Michael Mabrity, Barbara Mabrity, and their family members operated the light for about seventy years.

By the 1960s improved navigation systems, including radar and loran (later replaced with satellite navigation) and automated light systems, made many lighthouses obsolete. In 1966, the Key West Art and Historical Society took over the lighthouse keeper's quarters, setting up the museum. The lighthouse itself was decommissioned in 1969.

The lighthouse and the keeper's quarters were restored over a three-year period in the 1980s, and today the museum maintains exhibits telling the story of the Mabrity family and the light they kept burning. The quarters bungalow contains furniture, photographs, and exhibits that help convey the history of Key West.

BAHAMA VILLAGE

Bahamian fishermen and wreckers built temporary camps in the keys before the U.S. took over Florida, and Bahamians or "Conchs" were among the earliest settlers in Key West. The Bahamian heritage is commemorated in the Bahama Market in a neighborhood originally settled by Bahamians southwest of Whitehead Street. A sign over the entrance to Petronia Street off Duval Street marks the Village neighborhood.

This lively little market on the corner of Petronia and Whitehead Streets is in the Bahama Village neighborhood, west of Duval Street. Once a neighborhood of settlers from the Bahamas, in recent years, like much of Key West, the district has been gentrified, although wall murals and this market still evoke its heritage.

CHURCHES

Constructed in 1904, the Basilica of St. Mary Star of the Sea at the corner of Truman Avenue and Windsor Lane is directly descended from the first Catholic church in Key West. The name evokes "stella maris," a tradition that associates the Virgin Mary with the guiding star of mariners, the North Star.

A quiet courtyard at St. Paul's Church on Duval Street is graced with this statue.

The earliest settlers of Key West had to deal with storms, wrecks, and the struggle for survival against the hazards of the sea. The pioneer families sought solace in religion, building two impressive churches whose successors remain landmarks today. They are the Catholic Basilica of St. Mary Star of the Sea at the corner of Windsor Lane and Truman Avenue, and a few blocks away, St. Paul's Episcopal Church at 401 Duval Street.

Both churches, with their stories of survival, have served as beacons of faith through adversity. The first recorded mass in Key West was celebrated in 1846 by a visiting priest from Havana, in City Hall at the foot of Duval Street. However, as the number of Catholic families increased, a church was built in 1851. In 1901, the Key West Star of the Sea church was destroyed in fire, and the present Basilica was completed in 1904.

Just as the first Catholic church was destroyed, a similar fate met the Episcopal church. The first St. Paul's, built in 1838–1839, was demolished by a hurricane in 1846; the second St. Paul's burned to the ground in the Great Fire of 1886. (See "The 1886 Fire Mystery," page 79.) Then, the third St. Paul's fell to another hurricane in 1909. The current building, a solid concrete structure, opened for services in 1919. With its location on busy Duval Street, it hosts a steady stream of visitors.

At the corner of Eaton and Duval Streets, St. Paul's Episcopal Church demonstrates the survival of faith in the face of adversity: two earlier St. Paul's churches in Key West were lost to hurricanes and a third to fire.

2 Pioneers, Pirates, and Wreckers

In the decades from the 1820s through the 1850s, Key West played a crucial part in U.S. history. Like other frontier towns, Key West's first years were wrapped up with establishing legal claim to the land, ensuring law and order, and securing the new territory for the United States. On land in the "Wild West," the U.S. Army, county sheriffs, local courts, and federal marshals did the job; in Key West it was the navy and an admiralty court that brought peace and legal stability to the sea frontier off the southern tip of Florida.

Because of Key West's location, it was obvious that the city would be an important strategic spot when the United States acquired Florida. As the southernmost port city in the United States, and lying just 90 miles north of Spanish-held Havana, Cuba, Key West would be key to trade and security on the new southern frontier. For investors who recognized the potential, the first step was getting clear title to the land.

In 1815, Juan Pablo Salas, a Spanish artillery officer based in St. Augustine, received a deed from the Spanish government for Key

The sketch below of "The Business Part of Key West," looking north from the cupola on top of the Asa Tift Warehouse, just off Mallory Square, was done in 1838 by William A. Whitehead, brother of pioneer John Whitehead.

West. However, as the American aspiration for acquiring Florida became clear, Salas grew eager to sell the island. Salas sold the island at a meeting in Havana to John Simonton, a man with business connections in Mobile, Alabama. Simonton paid $2,000 for the deed. Despite the fact that Salas had previously sold the claim to another buyer, John Simonton prevailed as the rightful owner.

The Four Pioneers

Simonton then sold a quarter of the island to John Whitehead and another quarter to John Fleeming. A third quarter was later purchased by Pardon C. Greene. The claims of Simonton, Whitehead, Fleeming, and Greene were confirmed by the U.S. Land Claims Board on December 14, 1825, and reaffirmed in 1828 by an act of Congress. Whitehead made numerous sketches and plans of the developing town, which help document the early appearance of Key West.

Key West in Pirate History

In the wake of the Napoleonic wars and the U.S.-British War of 1812, many laid-off British and American seamen took up working as privateers for the independent nations of Latin America. Sailing on ships with "letters of marque" from the new republics like Mexico and New Grenada, privateers could legally seize Spanish ships and capture their cargoes, getting an award of prize money from the governments. Some privateers turned to piracy, attacking ships of all nations, often murdering the crews and passengers, taking the goods, and keeping or burning the vessels. By the early 1820s, the pirates of the Caribbean or "brethren of the coast" became a genuine threat all along the Gulf Coast of the United States and a hazard to shipping throughout the region.

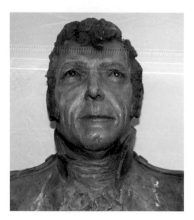

Commodore David Porter (1780–1843) commanded the "Mosquito Fleet" out of Key West, suppressing piracy in the Caribbean. He was court-martialed because he exceeded his orders with a landing in Puerto Rico, resigned from the U.S. Navy, and accepted command of the Mexican navy.

Navy and Key West

Faced with the piracy outrages, the U.S. Navy Department followed up on Perry's earlier recommendations, not only for lighthouses, but for a naval base, recognizing the strategic value of the location. In 1822, the navy ordered Commodore David W. Porter, a hero of the War of 1812, to set up a naval station at Key West, to cruise throughout the Caribbean, and to suppress pirates. From 1823 to 1825, Porter established the navy base and ruled the island under military control, much to the dismay of the merchants and businessmen who hoped to develop a commercial port. Porter organized the "Mosquito Fleet," so named for its small, fast ships that were ideal for pirate-chasing.

In 1823, Porter's Key West-based fleet consisted of eight schooners between 47 and 65 tons, each of which carried three guns and a crew of thirty-one men. The squadron also included five smaller river barges named *Gnat*,

Midge, Mosquito, Sandfly, and *Gallinipper* for chasing pirate boats into shallow water and up rivers and creeks, pursuing their crews directly to their inland hideouts. Porter sent the schooners and river barges on missions through the Caribbean, the Bahamas, and the Gulf of Mexico. His ships not only fought pirate ships at sea, they struck at pirate lairs ashore in Mexico, Cuba, and Puerto Rico. A historic marker at 625 Truman Street describes Porter's anti-piracy campaign.

Among the pirates Porter defeated was the Cuban pirate Diabolito, who sailed aboard the four-gun schooner *Catalina.* In 1823 sailors from two of the barges in Porter's fleet, the *Gallinipper* and the *Mosquito,* tracked down Diabolito off the northern coast of Cuba near

The Fajardo Incident

In October 1824, pirates raided Saint Thomas in the Danish Virgin Islands and then returned to their base in Fajardo, on the eastern tip of Puerto Rico, with $5,000 worth of property stolen from an American merchant. From Key West, Commodore Porter ordered Navy Lieutenant Charles Platt, in command of the USS Peacock, *to recover the trader's goods. Platt landed a small party in Fajardo on October 27. Platt and his shore party left their naval uniforms behind and wore civilian clothes. The Spanish apprehended Platt and his men and charged them with piracy, holding them prisoner for a day. Platt explained the situation, and the Spanish then released the American sailors.*

Hearing the details, Commodore Porter was outraged that a U.S. naval officer and sailors had been detained by local Spanish authorities. Porter sailed to Fajardo with a small fleet consisting of the John Adams, *the* Beagle, *and the* Grampus. *Porter landed a detachment of 200 sailors and marines, and spiked the Spaniards' cannons.*

Under threat of bombardment from Porter's ships, the local Spanish command made a public apology. Porter reported to the secretary of the navy, on November 15, 1824, that he had "no doubt our flag will be more respected, hereafter, than it has been, by the authorities of Porto Rico." Porter had acted without orders, and his peremptory "invasion" of Spanish territory and his demand for an apology far exceeded his orders. Summoned for court-martial, he resigned from the navy.

This statue of a pirate, inspired by legend and artists' imaginations, guards the staff entrance to the Mel Fisher Maritime Museum. Real pirates infested the Caribbean in the early 1820s until put out of business by the U.S. Navy operating out of Key West.

Judge William Marvin (1809–1902) operated the "wrecker court" in Key West from 1839 until 1863. After the Civil War, he briefly served as the appointed governor of Florida.

Matanzas. When the pirates abandoned ship, the American ships fired on the swimming pirates, exterminating dozens of them. Diabolito was killed in the action, and the survivors were captured by local Cuban villagers.

After resigning from the navy in 1825 (see "The Fajardo Incident"), Commodore Porter joined the revolutionary government of Mexico in 1826 as general of the marines—that is, head of the Mexican navy. For two years, Porter continued to use Key West as a base for his Mexican naval ships as he attacked Spanish ships, recruiting volunteers from stranded seamen in the port and from as far afield as New Orleans. Though no longer in the navy, Porter wrote to Congress in 1829 describing Key West as the "Gibraltar of the Caribbean" and the best location for a U.S. naval base south of the Chesapeake. Despite Porter's falling-out with Secretary Southard, the navy agreed and has kept a base in Key West to the present time.

Even after Porter's resignation from the U.S. Navy, the Key West-based Mosquito Fleet continued to strike against a few remaining pirates. One of the most important captures

Nineteenth Century Houses of Key West

Scattered throughout Key West are dozens of houses built in the nineteenth century. A number have been very carefully restored, and a few are open to visitors as museums. Some of the houses were built by ship's carpenters, using some techniques that helped preserve them: tight construction, attention to water run-off, and expert wood joinery methods. They were usually built with no paper plans, but simply based on memories of homes they had seen in their homeports or on their travels. Lumber was imported, either directly or from auctioned cargoes of wrecked ships.

A major fire in 1886 destroyed much of the downtown area, so very few homes from the "pioneer" era survive in their original form, although a number, such as those mentioned in this chapter, incorporate original early structures, later lovingly restored. Little has been preserved, but the restorations are sometimes meticulous and charming.

A stroll through back streets—such as Whitehead and Simonton Streets—is rewarded with glimpses into the past. On the residential streets, many homes are concealed behind lush foliage, revealing only hints of their Gothic Revival gables, Victorian trim, Queen Anne turrets, and other late nineteenth century features adapted to the local weather, such as tilting shutters, shaded porches, and airy balconies. Dozens of smaller cigar workers' homes, many of them "shotgun" cottages with the rooms arranged one behind the other, can be found scattered on side streets, some in clusters. As private residences or commercial establishments, most examples of nineteenth century architecture are not open to visitors, but even so, the restored buildings of the historic district are major attractions of the city and are listed in the appendix to this book.

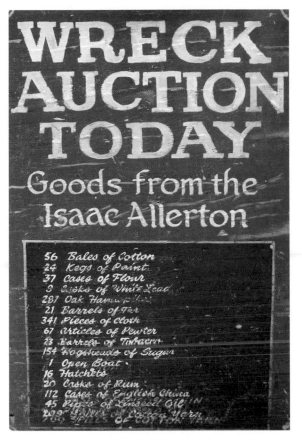

William A. Whitehead (1810–1884), a civil engineer, left some of the best descriptions of early life in Key West. Streets in the town were named for his sisters Caroline, Margaret, and Emma, and for his brother Thomas. John Whitehead, the eldest brother, was one of the original four pioneers who obtained a quarter of the island from John Simonton.

This Wrecker Auction Board on display outside the Shipwreck Museum replicates the list of goods auctioned by order of the wrecker court to convert salvaged cargo and ship equipment into cash for division among wreckers, owners, and insurance companies. For decades, the major business of Key West was ship salvage.

was made by Captain John D. Sloat, who arrested a legendary "Robin Hood" of Puerto Rican pirates, Roberto Confresi. Sloat turned Confresi over to Spanish authorities for trial and execution in 1825.

Wreckers and the Wrecker Court

Despite legends, there is no evidence that wreckers in Key West or elsewhere intentionally lured ships ashore with false lights or other means. In fact, wreckers often rescued stranded seamen and passengers (without financial reward), as well as salvaging ships and cargoes.

While wreckers had already operated from home bases in the Bahamas and from scattered camps in the Florida Keys before 1821, with the establishment of Key West, the wrecking business immediately flourished there. An 1824 newspaper report showed that wreckers brought some $14,000 worth of goods into town. The business grew rapidly. John Simonton reported that in the twelve-month period December 1824–December 1825, wreckers salvaged goods valued at more than $293,000. That is the equivalent of more than $5 million today.

Wreckers had an unsavory reputation, but when survivors or travelers encountered them, they were often pleasantly surprised. Dr. Benjamin Strobel, who met with John Audubon when he visited Key West in 1832, encountered some wreckers and described them at the time:

> The Captains were jovial, good humored sons of Neptune, who manifested every disposition to be polite and hospitable, and to afford every facility to persons passing up and down the Reef. The crews were composed of hearty, well dressed, honest looking men.

(Dr. Benjamin Strobel, *Charleston Courier,* May 4, 1837)

To regularize the salvage claims process, in 1828 the U.S. government established a superior court in Key West, empowered to handle admiralty cases. This meant that the local court could determine the exact legal amount that a wrecker could charge for services in hauling a grounded ship off a sandbar or reef, or for salvaging cargo from a wrecked ship. James Webb served as the first judge in the Key West Superior Court until 1838, when he retired to take up the position as secretary of state in the independent Republic of Texas. Judge William Marvin replaced Webb in the Key West court in 1839. Marvin became highly respected nationally, and he literally wrote the book on wrecking laws in 1858: *A Treatise on the Law of Wreck and Salvage.*

The wrecking business was the major source of the first private fortunes in the town and the primary reason that Key West thrived in

The Salt Business

From 1830 until the Civil War, Key West supplied a large proportion of the nation's salt, harvested from large drying pans. The demand for Key West salt fell off when inland salt mines were connected by the nation's growing rail network. A historic marker at 2100 Flagler Avenue details some of the early salt history.

Richard Fitzpatrick, a wealthy auctioneer for the ship wreckers' auctions, leased 100 acres of wetlands on the southeast end of Key West from John Whitehead in 1830. He set up drying pans with 2-foot coral rock walls and wooden floodgates to bring in seawater, which would then be evaporated, leaving the salt to be shoveled out in bushel baskets. Although he made good profits, Fitzpatrick gave up the business after four years. A number of other salt businessmen operated off and on until a hurricane in 1876 destroyed the business.

its first decades. Merchants and wholesalers bought up cargoes at auction, some to be reshipped, others to be consumed or purchased locally. Many of the homes of early businessmen, ship captains, auctioneers, and other prosperous Key West residents were fitted out with furnishings, tableware, kitchen equipment, paintings, and other valuables recovered by the wreckers and purchased at the local auctions.

In the years from 1830 through 1859, the steady flow of income from salvaged cargoes and the business they generated was supplemented with income from local products. Businessmen experimented with marketing tropical fruit, including limes, tamarinds, and breadfruit. Others made profits from collecting sea salt.

The streets of Key West echo the names of the pioneers, with Whitehead Street, Simonton Street, Greene Street, and Fleming Street (with spelling modernized from "Fleeming") all in the immediate vicinity of downtown. Southard

Sculptor James Mastin's wrecker monument ("The Wreckers") in the Sculpture Garden shows workers recovering cargo and rescuing survivors from a wreck ashore.

Street is named for Samuel L. Southard, secretary of the navy (1823–1829). Duval Street, laid out later, honors Governor William Pope Duval, the longest-serving governor of Florida (1822–1834). The stories of these and many of the town's other street names are told in the fascinating volume, *The Streets of Key West, A History through Street Names,* by J. Wills Burke.

WRECKERS MONUMENT

The centerpiece of the Key West Memorial Sculpture Garden, located off Mallory Square between Wall and Whitehead Streets, is the Wreckers Monument ("The Wreckers"). This sculpture depicts wreckers working to salvage goods from a ship washed ashore. The sculptor, James Mastin of Miami, took care to show that the wreckers not only salvaged cargoes, but also saved lives. The wrecker

Key West's Oldest House features a museum telling the story of Captain Francis Watlington and his family. Watlington was one of several Key West-based seafarers who made a fortune from the salvage business as wreckers.

on the left is shown with a small girl survivor clinging to his back as he rescues her from a ship awash on a reef or sandbar.

The peak years of the wrecking industry in Key West came in the 1850s. Improved lighthouses and lightships, better coastal charts, the planting of iron beacon markers, and the introduction of steam-powered ships, all tended to make nearby shipping somewhat safer. However, even with the aids to navigation and propulsion improvements, increased seagoing traffic and some intentional wrecks by owners hoping to collect insurance money meant the wrecking business thrived in the 1850s, before going into rapid decline during and after the Civil War (1861–1865).

Browsing through the Sculpture Garden, you will see busts of some thirty-six individuals who played important roles in various periods of Key West history. Among the busts, visitors will find several of the pioneers mentioned in this chapter.

OLDEST HOUSE
322 Duval Street

"The Oldest House" is a carefully preserved and restored historic site that serves to document the wrecker era. No other complete home in Key West pre-dates this structure.

Like many other early Key West settlers, the builder of the house, Richard Cussans, was originally from the Bahamas, born in Nassau in 1806. He built the house in the 1820s on a lot on Whitehead Street. The Historic American

The survival of the cookhouse behind the Oldest House is unique In Key West. However, throughout Florida, kitchens were often built in separate structures to reduce fire hazard to the home itself.

Building Survey dates the original building to about 1825.

The house was probably moved to its present spot at 322 Duval in the early to mid-1830s. The Key West Restoration Foundation notes that Cussans was a ship's carpenter, and he incorporated several maritime features into the building, including mortise and tenon joinery and a ship's hatch in the master bedroom roof that could be raised for ventilation. A striking feature of the front facade of the house is the three different-sized dormer windows.

An early resident of the house was Captain Francis Watlington and his wife and daughters, and the building is often referred to as the "Captaln Francis Watlington House." A sea captain engaged in the wrecking business,

Watlington served as harbormaster, customs inspector, and captain of the Sand Key lightship. Watlington's portrait along with a wrecker's license and rules of wrecking are on display in the house.

Watlington was elected to the Florida Legislature in 1859. During the Civil War, he served in the Confederate Navy, and after the war returned to Key West until his death in 1887. The house stayed in the family of Watlington descendants until 1972. In 1974, the house was purchased for restoration and preservation and management was turned over to the Old Island Restoration Foundation.

Behind the house, a quiet garden includes the only surviving outdoor cookhouse in Key West. The cookhouse was originally connected to the

This "Pirates Well" in front of the Captain George Carey House replicates the legendary freshwater well near the waterfront that drew pirates and others to the spot even before the first permanent settlement.

main house by a covered structure that provided some sleeping areas as well. In the days of wood-burning cookstoves, Florida kitchens were often built behind and separated from the main house because of the danger of fire. Today, Key West's Oldest House serves as a museum dedicated to the town's early history, with original furnishings, ship models, and documents telling the story of prosperity from wrecking. Admission to the house and gardens is free, and the building and gardens are open daily from 10 A.M. to 4 P.M., except Sundays, Wednesdays, and holidays.

CAPTAIN GEORGE CAREY HOUSE
410 Caroline Street

The home of Captain George Carey is reputedly the second oldest surviving house in Key West. Captain Carey, a colorful figure who claimed descent from William the Conqueror, ran a wholesale liquor business. Carey built the original two-room part of the house in the mid- to late 1830s. Over the nearly two centuries since, the house was expanded and remodeled, with the original two rooms moved to the rear.

Next door to the main house, facing the garden and set back from the street, is a small cottage

The Dr. Joseph Yates Porter House near the corner of Caroline and Duval Streets was built in 1839 and survived city fires and hurricanes. Dr. Porter was born and died in this home.

that was occupied by the poet Robert Frost during his winter visits over a sixteen-year period, 1945–1960. By 2014, the Carey House had become a real estate office.

Next to the front door of the main house is a well, representing the "Pirates Well" that supplied water to wreckers, turtlers (as the turtle fishermen were known), and pirates who stopped at Key West in the 1700s to refill their casks.

DR. JOSEPH YATES PORTER HOUSE
429 Caroline Street

This imposing mansion was built on land bought by Judge James Webb in 1837, just before he retired as first judge of the wrecker court in Key West and took up his position as secretary of state in the Texas Republic. The house itself was built in 1839 as a two-story house, purchased by Joseph Yates Porter, who had moved to Key West from Charleston. His son, Joseph Yates Porter Jr. was born in the house in 1847 (and he died in the same room, 80 years later, in 1927). The younger Porter became a well-known doctor.

Dr. Joseph Yates Porter Jr. was raised by his grandmother. He studied medicine at the Jefferson Medical College in Philadelphia, graduating in 1870. He served some nineteen years in the Army Medical Corps, including the post of acting assistant surgeon at Fort Jefferson

Dr. Joseph Yates Porter (1847–1927), as Florida's first state health officer, combined quarantine and fumigation in attacking yellow fever and other contagious diseases.

in the Dry Tortugas. One of his specialties was the study of yellow fever, which frequently struck Florida, the Bahamas, and Fort Jefferson as well. Porter was instrumental in the studies that led to the discovery that yellow fever was carried by mosquitoes, and he is credited with bringing an end to the quarantine of ships and burning of homes during yellow fever epidemics.

Dr. Porter's wife was the former Louisa Curry, one of the daughters of Key West pioneer William Curry, later known as the richest man in Florida.

AUDUBON HOUSE
AND TROPICAL GARDENS
205 Whitehead Street

Across the street from the Mel Fisher Maritime Museum, the Audubon House and Tropical Gardens includes tropical gardens, an herb garden, a gift shop and the Audubon House Gallery, and a nursery in the style of the 1840s. Included in the house are many first editions of the books by famed naturalist John James Audubon (1785–1851), including his most well-known work, *The Birds of America.* The house and the collections reflect his visits to Key West and the Dry Tortugas in 1832. One of the bird pictures in that book, the white-crowned pigeon, accounts for the designation of the building as the

John Audubon visited Key West in 1832 and painted this picture of the white-crowned pigeon. His assistant, George Lehman, painted the background geiger tree foliage. Geiger trees can still be found on the grounds of the Audubon House.

Audubon House. The painting used as its setting a rough-leaved cordia, or geiger tree, found in the yard at this address. It was the location of the home of Captain John Huling Geiger, Key West's first harbor pilot.

When demolition of the house was planned in the late 1950s, it was rescued by Mitchell and Frances Wolfson, who set up a foundation, the Audubon House Museum and Tropical Gardens, with $250,000 of their own funds in 1960. Architect Alfred Milton Evans directed the restoration of the house that now serves as a memorial to Audubon and his visit to Key West.

The rear balcony of the Audubon House overlooks a lush tropical garden.

SHIPWRECK TREASURES MUSEUM
1 Whitehead Street

The Key West Shipwreck Treasures Museum offers visitors a lively introduction to the world of wreckers, and the seamen, judges, auctioneers, and merchants who made salvage the first successful business of Key West in the period from the 1820s through the 1850s.

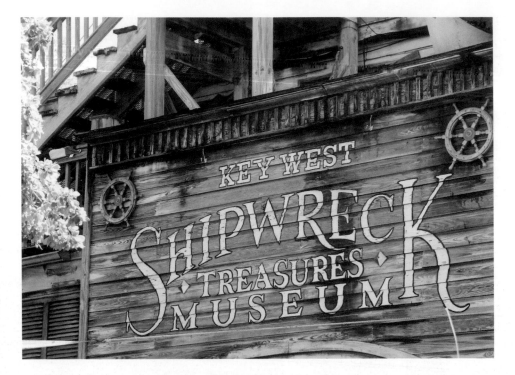

The Key West Shipwreck Treasures Museum houses hundreds of salvaged items and tells the story of the wrecker era.

Costumed interpreters give guided tours of the museum and its artifacts. The main room is modeled after the Tift Warehouse, which stands across the street from the museum and today houses numerous souvenir vendors.

Featured in the museum is the wreck and items of cargo of the *Isaac Allerton*. The *Isaac Allerton* sank 15 miles east-southeast of Key West near the Saddlebunch Keys on August 28, 1856, as the result of a hurricane. The *Isaac Allerton* was built in Portsmouth, New Hampshire, in 1838. By today's standards it was a tiny cargo ship–137 feet long and rated at 594 tons. Even so, Judge Marvin of the wrecker court estimated the value of the goods retrieved from the *Allerton* at $96,309, the largest amount recorded in the Key West wrecker hearings.

Among the items brought back from a modern salvage operation and on display today are ink wells, snuff bottles, cuff links, knives, pots, plates, toothbrushes, oil lamps, scales, brass candlesticks, navigation instruments, 1852 gold coins, bottles, and clay pipes. According to the ship's manifest, the ship carried large blocks of marble that were intended for the new floor of the U.S. Customs building in New Orleans. The museum's collection includes several large sections of the marble, including a one-ton piece displayed outdoors.

At the Shipwreck Treasures Museum, visitors can climb to the 65-foot lookout and view the city and harbor.

This display in the Shipwreck Treasures Museum shows the sorts of items salvaged from wrecks in the nineteenth century, including ink pots, a purser's stamp, household utensils, and trade goods.

PATTERSON-BALDWIN HOUSE
Corner of Duval and Eaton Streets

The Patterson-Baldwin House is now a financial services office. It is one of the oldest buildings in Key West, with parts of it tracing back to 1838. Originally a one-and-a-half-story cottage with a front and side porch, over the years it has been modified with elements of Classical Revival and Bahamian features. Alexander Patterson, who served as Key West mayor for three separate periods (1841–1842, 1848–

1852, and 1856–1857), built the house, but reputedly never occupied it. He had it moved to its present site in 1847 after a devastating hurricane hit the island.

The building once housed a school and lays claim to being the "Oldest Schoolhouse in Key West," as noted in the large marker on the corner of Duval and Eaton Streets. According to local historians, William Pinckney, the collector

The Key West Shell Warehouse at 402 Wall Street, now a mall of souvenir shops, once housed Asa F. Tift's icehouse. The story of Asa Tift, prominent wrecker and Connecticut-born Confederate patriot, is told here and across the square at the Shipwreck Treasures Museum.

The tower at the Shipwreck Treasures Museum, like the early cupolas and towers of the wreckers, provides a view of Key West, the harbor, and nearby keys and islets where sailing ships often ran aground.

**Before the Civil War, the Patterson-Baldwin House
housed a school presided over by Madame Passalogue.**

of customs, lived in the building, and it was a relative of his, Madame Passalogue, who taught classes in the building for some years.

In 1860, the home was bought by John P. Baldwin, a wealthy salvage operator who served as mayor of Key West for two back-to-back terms, 1857–1861. During the Civil War, Baldwin, a supporter of secession and the Confederacy, moved with his family to the Bahamas. Returning after the war, the Baldwins extended the original cottage, adding the two-story section now facing Duval Street. Descendents of John P. Baldwin continued to own the home well into the twentieth century. In 1962 they sold it to Joan and Edward B. Knight, who conducted the modern restoration.

3 Civil War: 1861–1865

Key West and its harbor would play a major role throughout the Civil War. The only way to reach Key West in the nineteenth century was by sea. Both the Key West U.S. Navy base and Fort Zachary Taylor were held by the Union military. Although most Key West civilians supported the secession of Florida from the Union, the Union military presence was far too strong to oppose. So, even though Florida joined the Confederacy, the island of Key West remained a Union-occupied enclave within the Confederacy throughout the war.

The Key West navy base would play a crucial role in the Civil War. The base helped enforce the so-called "Anaconda" blockade of the South, designed to prevent the export of goods (particularly cotton, cattle, and sugar) and the import of weapons and other strategic goods. With army and navy reinforcements, by the end of the war Key West was the most populous city in Florida.

Along the coast of Florida from south of Pensacola around to Cape Canaveral—the areas covered by the Key West-based blockade squadron—there were no major port cities. Even so, blockade runners from the Bahamas, Bermuda, Cuba, and smaller islands of the West Indies, operating in small, fast ships, conducted trade to and from smaller ports like Bradenton on the Manatee River, while places like Port Charlotte, a small port north of Fort Myers on the Gulf Coast, were used to ship out cattle to supply Confederate forces. Even though Florida did not have major ports, the Union Navy seized and brought into Key West a recorded 299 blockade-running ships, some powered by steam. By the end of the war, with confiscated ships moored thick in the harbor, the clustered masts looked like a forest.

The Anaconda Plan and Key West

Union General Winfield Scott proposed the "Anaconda Plan" to cut off the Confederacy from outside trade. The plan involved a blockade of the seaports in the Confederacy and then a campaign to cut the Confederacy into two parts by regaining control of the Mississippi River. With some modification, this grand strategy was used throughout the war. Key West played an important part in the plan, as the U.S. Navy based the Gulf Blockading Squadron in Key West, at first with responsibility for the whole Gulf Coast from Texas to Key West. In 1862, the command was split, with the East Gulf Blockading Squadron, based in Key West, responsible for enforcing the blockade from Pensacola around the coast of Florida up to Cape Canaveral on the Atlantic.

On occasion, U.S. naval officers operating out of Key West would mistakenly stop a Spanish ship bound for Cuba, much to the indignation of the Spanish officials. The rules of war did allow inspection of ships flying foreign flags on the high seas to determine if the flag usage was legitimate, but the stoppages still led to friction with the Spanish authorities. Union Secretary of the Navy Gideon

Welles and Secretary of State William Seward warned the Key West naval officers particularly to avoid chasing ships into Spain's territorial waters surrounding Cuba and Puerto Rico.

Commodore David W. Porter, who had set up the navy base in Key West, had two sons who followed him into the navy. One was Admiral David Dixon Porter. In February 1862, Admiral Porter assembled a fleet of gunboats, called the "Mortar Flotilla," at Key West for the attack on New Orleans that finally succeeded on April 29, 1862. The main attack up the Mississippi River to New Orleans was led by Admiral David Farragut, famous for the line, "Damn the torpedoes," in his attack on Mobile Bay. David Farragut was Admiral David Dixon Porter's adoptive brother.

Confederates in a Union City

When the citizens of Florida considered secession early in 1861, Key West residents had to decide on difficult questions of loyalty. Stephen Mallory, who had served as U.S. senator from Florida, resigned from the U.S. Senate on the secession of Florida in January 1861 and went on to work with the Confederate government in Richmond, Virginia, where he served as secretary of the navy.

Some Confederates who remained in Key West either quietly acquiesced to Union control of the city or grumbled about it. As in literally hundreds of cities and towns in Union-controlled regions of the United States, both North and South, military authorities closed pro-Confederate or outspoken newspapers critical

Admiral David Porter's flotilla set off from Key West for the Union attack on Confederate-held New Orleans on March 6, 1862. The schooners were equipped with heavy mortars for bombardment.

Key West in the Civil War: Chronology

March 1860
U.S. Navy captures three slave ships off Cuba and brings African refugees to Key West; housed in barracks at Higgs Beach.

November 1860
Abraham Lincoln wins presidential election.

December 1860–February 1861
Secession of seven southern states including Florida; formation of Confederacy. Key West remains in Union control.

April 12–13, 1861
South Carolina troops fire on Fort Sumter in Charleston Harbor, beginning Civil War.

April and May 1861
Four more states secede from the Union and join the Confederacy.

May 6, 1861
Gulf Blockading Squadron headquarters is established by U.S. Navy in Key West.

February 1862
The Union Navy East Gulf Blockading Squadron HQ is established in Key West; Admiral David D. Porter heads U.S. Navy assembly of the Mortar Fleet at Key West for the Union attack on New Orleans.

1862
East and West Martello Towers constructed at Key West.

April 9, 1865
General Robert E. Lee surrenders to U.S. General Ulysses S. Grant.

April 14–June 1865
Lincoln assassinated by J.W. Booth; four co-conspirators of Booth sentenced to prison terms in Fort Jefferson, in the Dry Tortugas off Key West.

March 1, 1869
Dr. Mudd and two surviving assassination conspirators pardoned and released from Fort Jefferson by President Andrew Johnson.

This view of navy ships off Key West from the East Martello Tower was published in *Harpers Weekly*, April 18, 1874.

of the Union government. In Key West, William Ward, editor of *Key of the Gulf*, published strong arguments for secession in May 1861. Threatened with arrest by the local Union Army, he fled the town and joined the Confederate service.

SITES

FORT JEFFERSON MUSEUM
Margaret Street

At the foot of Margaret Street in Key West is a small museum devoted to the history of Fort Jefferson on the Dry Tortugas. The fort itself can be reached by boat on a day trip. The Fort Jefferson Museum in Key West explains the history of the fort and its role as a prison for some of those involved in the Lincoln assassination.

On April 14, 1865, just five days after General Robert E. Lee surrendered the Army of Northern Virginia to Union General U.S. Grant, John Wilkes Booth shot Lincoln at Ford's Theater in Washington.

Although Booth was tracked down and killed while resisting arrest, eight co-conspirators

A diorama at the Dry Tortugas Museum at the foot of Margaret Street in Key West depicts Dr. Samuel Mudd treating a patient while serving his sentence at Fort Jefferson for his part in the plot to assassinate Abraham Lincoln.

were tried and convicted. Four were executed and four others were sentenced to life in prison and sent to Fort Jefferson.

The four imprisoned at Fort Jefferson included Dr. Samuel Mudd, who had treated Booth's broken leg and had delayed reporting his visit, giving Booth time to elude pursuit for twelve days. Two years after the arrival of Mudd and three other conspirators as prisoners at Fort Jefferson, a yellow fever epidemic swept the fort, killing some prisoners and staff, including the prison's doctor. Dr. Mudd took over duty as chief medical officer at the fort. That service received very favorable notice from the military. President Andrew Johnson, who had pardoned most of the Confederate government officials and military officers over the years 1865–1868, finally issued a pardon to Dr. Mudd at Fort Jefferson just a few days before leaving office in March 1869.

STEPHEN MALLORY BUST, MEMORIAL SCULPTURE GARDEN, AND MALLORY SQUARE

Mallory Square and a bust in the nearby Memorial Sculpture Garden commemorate Stephen Mallory. (See "Stephen Mallory and Charles Mallory.") Born in Trinidad in the British West Indies, his family moved to Key West in 1820, when Stephen was a young boy. When his father and older brother died, his mother operated a boarding house and sent Stephen off to school in Pennsylvania.

On his return to Key West, Mallory studied law under Judge William Marvin and had a distinguished career as a maritime attorney, Monroe County Collector of Customs, and a judge. He served as U.S. senator from Florida from 1850 until 1861, when he was appointed by Confederate President Jefferson Davis as the Confederacy's secretary of the navy.

Mallory brought an advanced approach to the Confederate Navy, ordering ironclad, steam-propelled warships, submarines, and innovative mines. Among other ships he planned were two ironclad river gunboats, the *Louisiana* and the *Mississippi,* both built near New Orleans.

At the end of the Civil War, Mallory resigned

his post. He was arrested by Union forces and imprisoned without trial from May 20, 1865, to March 10, 1866. After being released, he returned to Florida and resided in Pensacola, where he resumed the practice of law until his death in 1873.

CIVIL WAR MONUMENT
281 Front Street (Clinton Place)

Throughout the United States after the Civil War, many municipalities erected war memorials to those who died in the conflict. Typically, the monuments in the South were dedicated to the boys and young men who served and died in the Confederate cause. Of course, Key West was an exception to that rule, as the town remained in Union control. The local monument to Union forces is the "Navy Club" monument in the little triangle of park formed by Greene, Whitehead, and Front Streets. Built in 1866, it is the oldest such monument in Florida and the most southerly. It is dedicated to the Union soldiers who lost their lives during the war, many from yellow fever.

With a unique Key West twist to the story, the Union monument is surrounded by a Confederate fence. A small metal plaque on the fence states, "Erected by J.V. Harris, Confederate Veteran." Jeptha Vining Harris was a medical doctor from Charleston who served aboard the Confederate ship *Morgan* during the Civil War. He moved to Key West after the war and served for a period as customs inspector in the large red brick customs house that is now the Key West Customs House Museum, directly across from the little triangle park. For a period, Harris and his wife lived in the Customs House building. He later served as Key West superintendent of schools and built the imposing mansion that is now "The Southernmost House." (See p. 64.) So after a fashion, the small park and monument are dedicated to Americans who fought on both sides in the Civil War.

This monument was raised to honor the Civil War Union troops who served in Key West. The fence around the monument was put up by a dedicated Confederate. Only in Key West!

This marble monument In Bayview Park was put up in 1924 by the United Daughters of the Confederacy to honor Key West men and boys who fought on the Confederate side during the Civil War.

Many years later, in 1924, the Daughters of the Confederacy erected a plain arch commemorating the Confederates from Key West who died in the Civil War. It stands in Bayview Park, facing Jose Marti Drive.

FORT ZACHARY TAYLOR

Fort Zachary Taylor was built as part of the Third System of Fortifications of the United States. These forts, built in the period from the 1820s through the 1850s, were located on water approaches to the nation, guarding ports, on the shores of rivers, on harbor islands or peninsulas, or at strategic points on the coast. They were made of brick or masonry and featured mounted heavy artillery with ranges that outreached the guns aboard the warships of the day. The forts were also designed with landward defenses, making them nearly impregnable to armed attack from troops ashore. Several such forts played important roles in the Civil War, including Fort Sumter and Fort Moultrie in Charleston Harbor, South Carolina, Fortress Monroe in Virginia, and Forts Pickens, Clinch, Jefferson, and Taylor in Florida.

Fort Taylor was first begun in 1845 and was still under construction when President Zachary Taylor died on July 9, 1850, after only sixteen months in office. The fort was named for him shortly thereafter. Hurricanes in 1846, 1850,

The beach at Fort Taylor Park

and 1856 set back the construction schedule. By the outbreak of the Civil War in 1861, the fort was nearing completion. Originally it was some 440 yards from the shore, reached by an easily defended causeway. The 8- and 10-inch artillery weapons housed in protected brick casemates were a major defense for the port of Key West.

Fort Zach, as locals call it, was shaped like a trapezoid, with the narrow side facing the sea. Along the broad side, facing the shore, interior wooden-roofed barracks housed troops. The foundations were of coral rock and granite set in concrete. The outer walls were three stories high.

When the U.S. Navy Blockading Squadron brought in captured blockade-running ships, they were anchored within gunshot of the fort to prevent anyone attempting to recapture them for the Confederacy.

After the war, in 1865 and then again in 1875 and 1876, severe storms damaged the fort. The landward side filled in with sand, so that today one can approach the fort on a dirt pathway, with a shallow moat behind the fort the only remnant of the waterway that once protected the land approaches. Visitors may be surprised to see heavy concrete walls on two sides of the fort. These were added in the period from 1898 to 1905 and are painted black, a stark contrast to the original brick construction.

During the modernization at the end of the nineteenth and beginning of the twentieth centuries, many older weapons were buried. Some were recovered during restoration of the fort in the 1960s. Today, heavy Civil War era artillery on display in the vaulted casemates are actual surviving armaments from the period.

The black walls within
Fort Zachary Taylor
are concrete additions to
the original brick fort.

One of the largest
collections of Civil
War era guns ever
recovered was
found during the
restoration of Fort
Zachary Taylor. Some
have been remounted
in the casemates.

A narrow moat reflects the fact that Fort Zachary Taylor was originally set offshore, reached by a 720-foot bridge. Landfill now allows a footpath to the site.

EAST AND WEST MARTELLO TOWERS

Two smaller forts in Key West were constructed after the Civil War broke out, and both are active tourist sites today. The East Martello Tower, located at 3601 South Roosevelt Boulevard, near the airport, is operated as a museum by the Key West Art and Historical Society. Closer to town, at 1100 Atlantic Boulevard, is the West Martello Tower, operated as a display of tropical plants and as a historical site by the Key West Garden Club.

A "martello tower" is a raised gun tower, with one or more guns on the roof that could fire in any direction. Very few such towers were ever built in North America, so these two, modeled on coastal defensive towers in Italy, are quite rare. During the war the towers were manned with troops from Fort Taylor and a short rail line connected the towers with the fort.

The East Tower is in fairly good repair, with museum displays located in the gun casemate rooms of the outer wall facing the ocean, and the central tower open so that visitors can climb and view the panorama of Key West from the roof. Exhibits in the casemate rooms include artifacts from the Civil War, as well as "Robert, the haunted doll," whose story is told in labels and in books available from the bookshop at the museum entrance.

After the Civil War, bored soldiers stationed at Fort Taylor would use the West Martello Tower for target practice, reducing some of the walls to rubble. Furthermore, after the building was abandoned, local residents would "mine" the bricks from the building for use in patios and walkways. The West Tower now hosts lush tropical trees and flowering plants. The outer

The West Martello Tower features a lush tropical plant garden and display created by the Key West Garden Club.

The Civil War-era East Martello Tower now houses a small museum operated by the Key West Art and Historical Society.

casemate wall that remains at the entrance shows the brick construction methods used.

Both towers were abandoned shortly after the Civil War: the West Martello Tower in 1866 and the East Tower in 1873.

HIGGS BEACH BURIALS

Next to the West Martello Tower is a display explaining the capture by the U.S. Navy of three slave ships—the *Wildfire,* the *William,* and the *Bogota*—off Cuba in 1860. Some 1,400 Africans who had been bought in Africa for sale as slaves in Cuba were brought to Key West where they were fed and treated at a newly constructed barracks on Higgs Beach. About 296 of the rescued slaves died and were buried at the site. Some of the graves lie immediately under the now-paved memorial next to the West Martello Tower, and others were under the site of the tower. Later, when the tower was built in 1862, the newly buried bodies were disinterred and moved to locations nearby. Some 800 of the survivors were sent by the U.S. Navy to Liberia in West Africa, which had been established as a refuge for freed African Americans. A simple memorial and plaque at Higgs Beach explain the burial ground and its significance.

As noted by Corey Malcom, Director of Archaeology for the Mel Fisher Maritime Heritage Museum, the Higgs Beach burial ground should not be thought of as a "slave cemetery," but rather as a cemetery of African refugees, quite unique in that the rescued men, women, and children were being cared for before being

The African Cemetery records the story of rescued Africans who landed in Key West in 1860. Nearly 300 died and were buried near here. The graves were first discovered in 2002 using ground-penetrating radar.

returned to Africa. The graves remained nearly forgotten until research in 2002 and 2010 with ground-penetrating radar located the precise sites of the interments.

BELL FROM *SAN JACINTO* AT CUSTOMS HOUSE MUSEUM

A major international incident, recounted in all major textbooks about the Civil War, was the detention on November 8, 1861, of the British ship *Trent* by the USS *San Jacinto* under the command of Captain Charles Wilkes. Returning from a cruise against slave trading ships off Africa, the USS *San Jacinto* stopped the *Trent* and Captain Wilkes removed two emissaries of the Confederacy, James Mason and John Slidell, both headed for Europe. After a dangerous diplomatic crisis with Britain, President Lincoln ordered the release of Mason and Slidell. The *San Jacinto* was then reassigned to Key West, where it operated with the Gulf Blockading Squadron. The bell from the *San Jacinto* is on display in the Key West Customs House Museum.

This bell is from the USS *San Jacinto*, the U.S. naval ship that stopped the British ship *Trent* in 1861 on the high seas, bringing the United States and Britain to a diplomatic crisis early in the Civil War.

ASA TIFT BUST, MEMORIAL SCULPTURE GARDEN

There are several reminders of Asa Tift scattered around Key West. A marker inside the door to the Shell Warehouse across from the Shipwreck Museum details Tift's life.

Prior to the Civil War, Asa F. Tift ran the largest salvage operation in Key West, where he maintained a large warehouse for salvaged goods next to Mallory Square. After moving to Mobile during the war, Asa and his brother Nelson Tift oversaw the design and financed the building of a ship, the *Mississippi,* for the Confederate Navy in New Orleans.

The Tifts agreed to work for the cost of materials only, and were given a free hand to modify the plans as they went along. The Tifts set up the works in the town of Jefferson, on the Mississippi River about two miles upstream from downtown New Orleans, beginning work on October 14, 1861. As the work continued on the CSS *Mississippi,* modified plans called for twenty guns and a longer keel. Unfortunately for the Tifts (and for the Confederacy), construction went slowly—it was hard to get materials, and labor supply was short due to the drafting of young men into the Confederate Army.

Union Secretary of the Navy Gideon Welles knew of the building of the two monster ironclads at New Orleans, and the two gunboats were part of the reason for the seizure of New Orleans by Admirals Farragut and Porter. When the Union Navy arrived at the riverside shipworks, the ironclad *Mississippi* still had another few weeks to go. On April 25, 1862, as Union forces approached, the Tifts had the still-incomplete ship burned. When the Tifts were later court-martialed for destroying the ship, they proved they had followed orders. Asa Tift returned to Key West after the war. In 1870 he built the house later occupied by Ernest Hemingway.

Asa Tift's plans for the CSS *Mississippi* show some of the innovative warship ideas developed by the Confederate Navy during the Civil War.

Asa F. Tift (1812–1889), a wealthy Connecticut-born Key West wrecker, nearly finished a major warship, the CSS *Mississippi,* for the Confederate side during the Civil War.

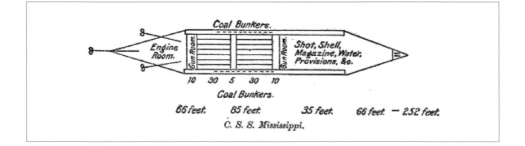

4 Age of Enterprise: 1866–1900

Key West expanded and thrived in the years after the Civil War, benefiting from improved transportation, as did much of the rest of the nation. As shipping and rail connections improved, linking Florida to the rest of the country, more and more enterprising businessmen in Florida grew wealthy by producing or harvesting a local product cheaply and selling it throughout the nation or overseas to markets where no one could turn out the product at any price. The same effect of the transportation revolution came to Key West, not by rail, but by sea.

Rail tracks did not reach the island until January 1912. Instead of rail connections, steam-shipping lines with scheduled stops in Key West linked the town with national and international markets in the years following the Civil War. From Key West, pineapples, sponges, turtle soup, and cigars all made local fortunes in the age of enterprise, and the newly rich entrepreneurs built grand homes in town, some of which survive to the present.

In 1873 the Connecticut- and New York-based Mallory Line offered passenger and freight service from New York to Key West and Galveston. Starting in 1876, the Mallory ships also started delivering mail to ports along the Atlantic and Gulf Coasts. Charles H. Mallory—no relation to Stephen Mallory (see page 43)—had first used sailing ships whose average travel time each way from New York to Key West was nine days, but with steam power, the trip took only four days. The Mallory Line ran six ships to keep up the service in the 1890s. A marker at 402 Wall Street in Key West commemorates the Mallory Line and its routes.

Another shipping line was started by Henry Plant in 1887, running from Tampa to Key West and on to Havana, with two ships, the *Mascotte*

and the *Olivette*. Through the 1890s the two ships made stops in Key West on a regular schedule. In the early 1900s, the *Olivette* was known as the fastest steamship in coastal service in the United States.

Railroad and shipping magnates Henry Plant and Henry Flagler competed through the period, with Plant's Atlantic Coast Line trains traveling from the North to Tampa, and Flagler pushing his East Coast Line south along the Atlantic Coast from St. Augustine to Miami by 1896. Archer Harmon, another entrepreneur, developed a project in 1895 to run a steamship line from the projected southern rail terminus of Flagler's East Coast Line in Miami to Key West, chartering the *City of Richmond*, renamed the *City of Key West*.

When the Harmon business faltered, Flagler took over the shipping line and operated it until 1900. In that year, Flagler organized the Peninsular and Occidental Steamship Company. The P&O line soon acquired the Plant ships and operated the *Mascotte, Olivette, Miami,* and *City of Key West*. The *Mascotte* and *Olivette* made three round trips a week from Key West to Havana during the high season of January through March.

The shipping line connections linked Key West to the markets for local businesses. Great fortunes were built from harvesting sponges, canning turtle soup, making cigars, and from marketing and shipping products from growers on other islands in the Florida Keys.

Pineapples

Although the precise origins of pineapple farming in the Keys have been hard to trace, one of the earliest pineapple plantations was started by Captain Ben Baker, who operated the wrecking ship *Rapid* from Key West. By the mid-1860s, Baker ran pineapple plantations on Plantation Key and Key Largo. Adolphus and Cephus Pinder opened a canning factory in the Keys to can pineapples in the 1880s. The site was just east of today's Cheeca Lodge on Islamorada. Plantation Key was named for its pineapple plantations.

Several varieties of pineapples, including the Sugar Loaf, Queen, Red Spanish, and Abbakkas, were raised in the Keys and marketed along with a wide variety of other fruits and vegetables. The harvests were shipped in small boats to Key West, then sent on to markets in other states by the steamship lines.

By the 1880s, pineapple shipments from the Keys through Key West ran over $200,000 per year. The opening of the railroad connection to Key West in 1914 spelled the end of the Florida Keys pineapple production, as pineapples from Cuba, brought by ship to Key West and shipped by rail on Flagler's Florida East Coast line, undercut the local prices.

Although the Keys' pineapple plantations are long gone, the emblem of the pineapple is found throughout Key West, a symbol of this aspect of Key West heritage: a Pineapple Bar is at the Southernmost Beach Cafe, a guest house known as Pineapple Cottage is at 1019 Whitehead Street, another known as the Perfect Pineapple is at Southard and Margaret Streets, and a gift shop called the Green Pineapple is at 1130 Duval. The Key West Winery at 103 Simonton produces a pineapple wine, and Key West bartenders are happy to produce a variety of pineapple cocktails.

Sponges

The Key West sponge business rose and fell in the period from 1887 to about 1900. But the competing Greek divers based in Tarpon Springs, Florida, using rubberized deep-sea diving suits with bronze spherical helmets, soon surpassed the Key West spongers. By 1905, some 500 divers worked out of Tarpon Springs, virtually ending the Key West business.

In Key West, the divers, mostly Bahamians, would simply hold their breath, dive down as deep as 25 feet, cut sponges from the sea-bottom, and harvest them. Today, there are only faint reminders of the once-thriving Key West sponge business.

SITES

TURTLE KRAALS

In the 1860s and 1870s one of the food fads that periodically sweeps the United States benefitted Key West but resulted in a severe endangerment of a species. Green turtle soup, which had become popular in Britain, came to be regarded as a gourmet specialty representing an elegant lifestyle. By 1880, there were ten turtling schooners operating out of Key West, according to Alison Rieser, author of *The Case of the Green Turtle, An Uncensored History*.

An American businessman and former chef, Armand Granday, capitalized on the fad and set up a turtle canning business in Key West in 1890. Even though Granday claimed all the turtles came from waters near Key West, most were captured off Nicaragua or on the beaches of Costa Rica, where they nested. Captured and kept alive on schooners, the turtles were brought to Key West and unloaded to seawater pens. Some of these "turtle kraals," now in disrepair, can be viewed next to the Turtle Kraal Restaurant at the foot of Margaret Street.

A whimsical "Spongeman" greets shoppers at the Sponge Market off Mallory Square.

Granday emphasized that the turtles were cooked immediately after being slaughtered, guaranteeing that the turtle meat was fresh. He claimed that "what champagne is to other wines, turtle is to other meats."

The canning business thrived, but the green sea turtle became an endangered species. Fortunately for the turtles, the fad finally wound down by the 1920s, according to naturalist Archie Carr.

The Turtle Kraals Restaurant and Bar recalls the heyday of turtle soup-making in Key West.

This label from Key West turtle soup recalls a local business that thrived from the 1890s to the 1920s. Today, the remnants of "turtle kraals" (enclosures for keeping live turtles) can still be seen at the foot of Margaret Street.

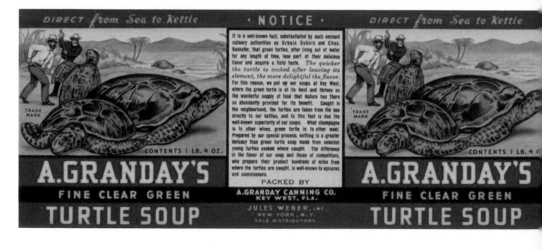

Eduardo Gato (1847–1926) was a successful cigar manufacturer in Key West and a leader of the Cuban-American community in the first decades of the twentieth century.

EDUARDO GATO SITES

Eduardo Gato (1847–1926), like some other famous immigrants to the United States in the nineteenth century, combined his energy and ambition to make a fortune and use it to aid his homeland. Around Key West several monuments, markers, and buildings are tangible reminders of Gato's career and his place in history.

As an eight-year-old boy in Cuba, Eduardo Gato walked miles to Havana to work in a cigar factory. During the upheavals of the Cuban revolution against Spanish rule, he emigrated to New York, where he continued to work in cigar factories. In 1874, he moved to Key West to start a factory, which occupied a building at the corner of Simonton and Amelia Streets. When that factory fell to flames in 1915, he built another factory there that opened in 1920.

At its peak in the 1890s, the Gato Key West Cigar Factory employed some 500 workers rolling and packing cigars. To provide housing for the workers, Eduardo Gato had forty small cottages built in the neighborhood, soon known as *El Barrio de Gato,* or "Gatoville." Several of the homes survive as modern cottages, and

a small park with a replica facade of a cigar worker's cottage stands at 616 Louisa Street, behind the parking lot and drive-up banking terminals of the First State Bank. The facade, park, and huge replica cigar in the mini-park are dedicated to this era of Key West and Cuban history. Gato's construction of worker housing reflected a national trend, as major entrepreneurs of the late nineteenth and early twentieth centuries often bought land, built homes for workers, and charged a nominal rent while retaining ownership of the property.

Gato succeeded, becoming a Key West civic leader. When the Board of Trade of Key West (an early version of the Chamber of Commerce) was established in 1885, he was elected as one of three vice-presidents of the organization. In his Key West factory, "lectors" or readers would read newspapers, literature, and pamphlets to the workers. As protests against Spanish rule in Cuba mounted, the lectors would read of Spanish atrocities and the cruel rule over the Cuban homeland. By some accounts, funds raised by Gato and his workers (who would donate a portion of their wages) provided crucial cash to the

Key West Cigars

The production and sale of cigars has been one of the most long-lasting enterprises in Key West. The cigar-making industry was introduced into Key West by William Wall in 1831, employing Cuban expatriates and immigrants. However, the Key West cigar industry began to flourish in the years after 1868, using tobacco imported from Cuba aboard the newly established steamship lines and employing refugees from the Cuban struggle for independence. Soon Key West cigars, using "Vuelta Abajo" tobacco from Cuba, were the highest-ranked cigars produced in the United States. The cigars sold at a price lower than imported Cuban cigars made in Havana. Among many other reminders of Key West's cigar history are the Cayo Hueso y Habana museum in the William Wall Warehouse at 410 Wall Street, the sites commemorating Eduardo Gato, such as the Gato Factory and the "Gatoville Park," and a marker noting the original location of the Luis Martinez Cigar Company at 2010 Staples Street between Second and Third Streets.

Cigar-making is still practiced in stalls on Duval Street.

struggle for liberation in Cuba. The lector tradition had started in Havana and continued to be very much alive in Florida tobacco factories, both in Tampa and Key West, into the 1930s.

Around 1890, Gato built a large home for himself and his family on Truman Avenue, where Bayview Park now stands. According to local legend, he brought in carpenters from Cuba to construct the building, which had a distinctive interior courtyard. In 1911,

Above:
The Gato Cigar Factory, which once employed 500 Cuban cigar workers, now houses Marion County offices at the corner of Simonton and Amelia Streets.

Right:
At the Gatoville Pocket Park, a display includes this mock-up of the front of a worker's cottage.

Near the Gato factory there are many former cigar workers' cottages like this one, now remodeled into comfortable, modern private residences or timeshares.

he dedicated the home to a Cuban-American committee in the City of Key West to serve as a hospital for the poor, naming it Mercedes Hospital, after his wife. When the city constructed Bayview Park at the site, the building was moved around 1919 to its present location at 1209 Virginia Street, where it continued to operate as a hospital until just before World War II. It was later sold and became a small apartment house and is now on the National Register of Historic Places.

MANSIONS

Four of the nineteenth century entrepreneurs' grand homes that can be seen today are the Peacon House at 712 Eaton Street, the Curry Mansion at 511 Caroline Street, the Key West Woman's Club at 319 Duval Street, and the Southernmost House at 1400 Duval.

The Peacon House, with its octagonal style, was built around 1885 for Richard Peacon (1840–1914), who owned Key West's leading

The Peacon House reflects Key West's rich architectural heritage.

grocery store, located at 800 Fleming Street. His parents had emigrated to Key West from the Bahamas. Peacon later became a founding director of the Island City National Bank. The Richard Peacon House is not eight-sided, but is called an "octagonal" house because it has a multi-faceted extension, which you can see from the street. In 1980, world-famous designer

Above: The Curry Mansion, at 511 Caroline Street, just off Duval Street, is now a popular guesthouse. The lobby houses a collection of antiques from the 1890s.

Below: The Wall Warehouse was built about 1879 at 410 Wall Street, just off Mallory Square. The warehouse and street are named for William Wall.

The Key West Woman's Club once housed Key West's first library. The building was originally the 1890s home of William Curry's daughter Eleanor and her husband, Martin Hellings, who supervised the important ocean telegraph link to Cuba.

Calvin Klein bought the house and then sold it in 1987. There is second Key West octagon style house two blocks to the northwest at 620 Dey Street, making the Peacon House the "southernmost octagon house" in the United States. Neither octagon house is open to visitors, but tourists often view them from tour trolleys or from the sidewalk.

One block north of Duval Street at 511 Caroline Street stands the stately **Curry Mansion Inn**. The building captures many elements of Key West's early prosperity. Started by William Curry in 1855, the building was finished in the 1890s by his son, Milton Curry. Furnished in 1890s style, the building's history reflects the lives of Key West's nineteenth-century entre-preneurs and civic leaders. Architecturally, the house combines elements from Rhode Island, New Orleans, and the Bahamas.

William Curry was born on Green Turtle Key in the Bahamas of Loyalist parents, and emigrated to Key West in 1837. He worked for about eighteen months for a merchant firm, then went to work for the U.S. Quartermaster, serving aboard a U.S. naval ship during the Seminole War. Returning to Key West, he went to work for William Wall.

In 1843, Curry married Euphemia Lowe, the daughter of Captain John Lowe, a Key West wrecker. In 1845 Curry entered the lucrative wrecking business in partnership with G.L. Bowne. When Bowne retired from the business in 1861, Curry, together with his father-in-law, owned (fully or in partnership with others) a small fleet of sloops and schooners engaged in the wrecking business. Over the next decades, Curry's business extended to ice manufacture, bonded warehouses for the importation of

Cuban tobacco, general merchandising, and ship equipment supply or "chandlery."

Two of William Curry's sons-in-law, Martin L. Hellings and Dr. Jeptha Vining Harris, also built mansions that survive to the present. Martin Hellings, who married Eleanor Curry, was manager of the International Ocean Telegraph Company. He built a mansion at 319 Duval Street about 1892.

After Hellings' death in 1908, the home was converted into an office building. In 1940 the **Key West Woman's Club** bought the building and, using ground floor rooms, operated the only Key West public library until the opening of the Monroe County Library in 1959. A carriage house in the rear of the grounds, built in the Hellings era, now houses the 88-seat Red Barn Theater.

The Southernmost House at 1400 Duval was built in 1896 for a cost of $250,000 as a private home for Dr. Jeptha Vining Harris, who had married Florida Curry. Dr. Vining Harris had served as a Confederate assistant surgeon during the Civil War. As noted earlier (p. 44), Harris funded the iron fence around the Civil War Monument across from the Customs House. Harris became customs collector and lived at first in the Customs House. He also resumed his medical practice after the end of the Civil War. He believed in promoting and improving public education, and he became the city's school superintendent. Harris School, which was built in 1905–1909 at 812 Southard Street, was named for him.

Later, the Southernmost House changed hands several times. During the Prohibition era, the Southernmost House building served as an elegant speakeasy. Then in 1939 the building became a Cuban-style nightclub called Café Cayo Hueso, with a notorious gambling club. Visitors included Ernest Hemingway, Truman Capote, Louis Armstrong, and Charles

The Southernmost House, one of the grand mansions from the 1890s, is now a fine inn.

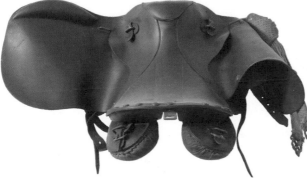

Ernest Hemingway's saddle is on display in the Southernmost House.

Lindbergh. On display on the first floor is Hemingway's saddle, a reminder that he once went riding using horses stabled in what is now the gift shop next door.

In the period from 1954 to 1996 the building was again a private home. Hilario and Placeros Ramos, from Spain, hosted many guests, including Presidents Harry S. Truman, Richard Nixon, John Kennedy, Dwight D. Eisenhower, and Jimmy Carter, as well as the King of Spain. In the mid-1990s, the next generation of the Ramos family, Charles and Mathilde Ramos, spent $3 million on renovations, turning the elegant Queen Anne building into an 18-room hotel. Charles Ramos had been elected mayor of Key West at age 24 in 1961, and became a leader in the city's historic restoration and preservation movement.

A brown pelican (*Pelicanus occidentalis*) swims just off the concrete pier at the southern end of Duval Street.

CABLE HUT

At the end of South Street, on the corner of Whitehead Street, a small, unobtrusive white structure reflects another bit of history from the era. The little concrete building represents the terminus of the first international undersea telegraph cable, completed in 1867 connecting Cuba and the United States. It opened with a message of greeting from U.S. Secretary of State William Seward to the Spanish governor of Cuba. The cable was operated by the International Ocean Telegraph Company. The small white concrete hut was completed in 1917 to protect the point where the cables from Cuba come ashore. At low tide it is possible to see the cables stretching out to the south.

The cable hut next to the Southernmost Point Buoy at South and Whitehead Streets is the point where the cables from Cuba come ashore.

The engraving above shows the installation of the
overseas cable from Cuba to Key West in 1867.

5 Cuba Libre: 1890s–1910s

The Spanish, who had lost all of their colonies on the mainland of North, Central, and South America by the 1820s, still held tenaciously to their colonies in Cuba and Puerto Rico, using troops to keep those two islands under tight control, arresting and imprisoning or exiling any who spoke out for independence. Political refugees and job-seekers fled Cuba through the nineteenth century.

Cubans in the United States who sought Independence from Spain organized a number of "filibustering" expeditions. Among the most well known of those early attempted revolutionary invasions were two led by Narciso López in the early 1850s. After the failure of the first attempt in 1850, López retreated to Key West. During another invasion attempt in 1851, he and his forces were captured and executed by Spanish authorities.

In Cuba, the Ten Years War (1868–1878) was a more serious and widely supported move for independence, particularly in the eastern end of Cuba. Although the movement failed, it produced leaders who continued the struggle in exile. In Key West, supporters of Cuban independence gathered at San Carlos Hall on November 9, 1878, to form the *Club Revolucionario Cubano de Cayo Hueso*. In December, Key West Cuban women formed another organization, *Club Hijas de Libertad*—"Daughters of Liberty." The organizations stayed in touch with corresponding organizations in New York City.

With the advent of inexpensive Havana-Key West steamship routes, the Cuban population in Key West increased. The émigrés brought cigar-making to Key West, as well as their passion for Cuban independence. With funding from cigar workers in New York and Key West,

in 1879 another expedition made up of exiled Cubans tried to land in Cuba and link up with rebels there, but that effort failed. This so-called 1879 *Guerra Chica* ("Little War") made it clear that better funding and organization were needed.

This bust of José Martí (1853–1895) in Bayview Park commemorates the father of Cuban independence. Martí visited Key West many times.

After the failure of the *Guerra Chica,* more and more Cubans emigrated to the United States, many joining compatriots in Key West and New York in the early 1880s. By the 1890s, Key West had the largest Cuban colony in the United States, numbering some 12,000. Some of the refugees opened small cigar stores or factories, while others joined the staff of *El Yara,* a Spanish language paper in Key West that supported the independence movement. Copies of the paper were regularly smuggled back into Cuba from Key West.

José Martí, the foremost intellectual leader of the movement for Cuban independence, visited Key West several times. Martí is recognized throughout Latin America as one of the major intellectual leaders of the late nineteenth century. The memorials to Martí in Key West recall the era when Cubans living in the United States helped popularize their cause and gave up hard-earned dollars to fund the liberation of the island from Spanish rule.

Martí was born in Cuba. As a teenager, he was arrested and imprisoned for advocating independence from Spain. Exiled to Spain, he continued his education and continued to write. Over his lifetime, his various newspaper editorials, essays, articles, poems, dramas, and other writings amounted to several thick volumes of work. For most of his life he lived in exile from Cuba, working to advance the cause for Cuban independence from Mexico, Guatemala, and the United States.

When he visited Key West on January 5, 1892, Martí met with other representatives of the Cuban émigré community there. The meeting voted for the *Bases del Partido Revolucionario* ("Basis of the Cuban Revolutionary Party"). Martí worked to raise support and funds for the party by visiting tobacco factories in Key West and Tampa, winning further supporters. From 1892 to 1894, Martí continued to raise

Explosion of the USS *Maine*

At 9:40 on the evening of February 15, 1898, an explosion on the U.S. Navy battleship Maine *rocked Havana, Cuba, where the ship was docked. More than 260 men lost their lives. Some 19 to 24 unidentified bodies recovered from the* Maine *were brought to Key West and buried in the Key West Cemetery, the closest U.S. cemetery to Havana. A U.S. Navy investigation at the time concluded that a mine had been set off beneath the ship, although later studies, including one by Admiral Hyman Rickover in the twentieth century, pointed to accidental causes, including a possible coal-dust explosion.*

However, in 1898 American public opinion held that the Spanish were to blame. On April 11, 1898, President William McKinley, under pressure, got Congressional approval to intervene in Cuba in favor of independence from Spain. After the U.S. set up a blockade of Cuba on April 21, Spain declared war on the United States. The U.S. Congress passed a formal declaration of war against Spain on April 25. The war lasted until August 1898. As a result Cuba received independence, while the United States acquired Puerto Rico, Guam, and the Philippines from Spain. The destruction of the Maine *had tipped public opinion to support armed intervention in favor of Cuban independence.*

support among Cuban exiles in the United States and other countries, including the Dominican Republic, Costa Rica, and Mexico. After extensive planning, recruiting, fund-raising, and an aborted expedition from Fernandina, Florida, Martí and other leaders began the uprising in Cuba in February 1895. Documents and photos on display in the El Meson de Pepe restaurant at 410 Wall Street, just off Mallory Square, give details of Martí's life and work.

Soon after arrival in Cuba, Martí was shot and killed at the battle of Dos Rios, May 19, 1895. After his death, verses from several of his poems were adapted as "Guantanamera" and became an informal Cuban national anthem.

The Spanish authorities reacted to the uprising with brutality, executing captured rebels, establishing areas for forcibly "reconcentrating" (the origin of the term "concentration camp") rural citizens—referred to as *reconcentrados*—to prevent them from aiding the rebels, and using modern weapons against the ill-equipped rebels. The revolution faltered but stayed alive, attracting wide support in the United States, partly due to lurid tales of Spanish atrocities published in competing Hearst and Pulitzer newspapers. Some of the stories were true.

Spanish-American War

After a three-month war between the United States and Spain in 1898, Cuba was liberated and gained its independence.

Despite its proximity to Cuba, Key West could not serve as a major port for embarkation of U.S. troops. Without road or rail connection from the mainland to Key West, troops and equipment could only get to Key West by sea. With its rail connection, Tampa became the major port for troops to assemble and board ships. Even so, Key West played a part in the war.

The sisters of the Convent of Mary Immaculate volunteered the use of their building to the navy to serve as a hospital, an offer gladly accepted. With the sisters acting as nurses, the convent-hospital treated more than 500 sick and injured from the war. The navy captured Spanish ships and brought 34 of them into Key West and held some 444 crew members and passengers from those ships as prisoners of war at Fort Taylor.

Cuba Libre and Daiquiri

Two popular alcohol cocktails came out of the Spanish-American War, and were popularized in Key West.

Cubans demanded freedom in a movement whose cry was "Cuba Libre!" Coca-Cola had been invented in 1886, and the popular drink of rum and Coke is known throughout Latin America as a "Cuba Libre." According to the Bacardi rum company, the name was invented shortly after the Spanish-American War:

> *One afternoon, a group of off-duty soldiers from the U.S. Signal Corps were gathered in a bar in Old Havana. Fausto Rodriguez, a young messenger, later recalled that Captain Russell came in and ordered Bacardi (Gold) rum and Coca-Cola on ice with a wedge of lime. The captain drank the concoction with such pleasure that it sparked the interest of the soldiers around him. They had the bartender prepare a round of the captain's drink for them. The Bacardi rum and Coke was an instant hit. ... When they ordered another round, one soldier suggested that they toast ¡Por Cuba Libre! in celebration of the newly freed Cuba. The captain raised his glass and sang out the battle cry that had inspired Cuba's victorious soldiers in the War of Independence.*

The daiquiri, made with rum and lime juice, is another cocktail that came out of the Spanish-American War—invented by an American mining engineer in the town of Daiquiri, Cuba.

In later years, the daiquiri was a favorite drink of Ernest Hemingway.

With the victory over Spain in August 1898, suddenly the United States acquired an overseas empire, with Puerto Rico, the Philippines, and Guam ceded to the United States, and with temporary occupation of Cuba (as well as a permanent base there at Guantanamo). The Spanish-American War demonstrated how long it took to bring U.S. warships from the Pacific to the Atlantic, spurring support for building a canal across Panama under U.S. control. Key West, with its naval base, was the most southerly station for the fleet and closest to the proposed canal.

Flagler's Over-Sea Railroad

As the nation faced the consequences of its new "empire," Henry Flagler, the developer of Florida's East Coast Railway, recognized the importance of establishing a land route to Key West. As the southernmost naval base in the United States and the closest to Cuba and to the soon-to-be completed Panama Canal, it was important to be able to move naval personnel, troops, coal, armaments, and supplies to Key West. Furthermore, Flagler was angry that his railroad competitor, Henry Plant, had reaped the rewards of publicity and funding during the use of Tampa as the jumping-off point for the U.S. invasion of Cuba in 1898. So in 1905 Flagler began the Over-Sea Railroad connection from Miami to Key West, completing the line in 1912. Little remains today of the Flagler railroad, since it was destroyed in a hurricane in 1935. However, for those who drive to Key West over Highway 1 from near Miami, some of the ruined railroad bridges can still be seen, paralleling the highway route. In Key West itself, Flagler built Trumbo Point, using landfill to create a terminus for the rail line and an embarkation point for ferries to Havana.

Labor Day Hurricane

The 1935 Labor Day hurricane was the strongest known hurricane ever to hit the United States, and has since been classified as a Category 5 hurricane, with winds up to 185 miles per hour. After starting as a tropical storm on August 29 in the Atlantic east of the Bahamas, the storm became a hurricane on September 1. Most of the casualties in the Keys resulted from a failed rescue attempt when a train was sent from Miami to evacuate Works Progress Administration (WPA) construction workers. Many of the workers were World War I veterans and their families, living in makeshift camps in Windley Key and Lower Matecumbe Key. On Labor Day, September 2, the rescue train was almost completely swept off the tracks, with only the engine surviving at Upper Matecumbe Key. The storm surge and debris killed more than 200 veterans in the work camps, and whole sections of the Florida East Coast Railway were destroyed beyond repair. Total casualties from the storm exceeded 400 killed. Ernest Hemingway published in the left-leaning New Masses *magazine a scathing denunciation of government policy that had sent World War I veterans to work in the Florida Keys during the hurricane season.*

SITES

FLAGLER STATION

A replica Flagler Station at the foot of Margaret Street, complete with a climate-controlled railroad car, contains artifacts, mementos, documents, and photographs telling the story of the Over-Sea Railroad.

JOSÉ MARTÍ AND LA TE DA

There are several reminders of José Martí in Key West, notably the statue of him in Bayview Park and the building known as "La Terraza de Martí," where he had addressed a crowd of thousands from the balcony of what was then the home of cigar manufacturer Teodoro Lopez.

Flagler Station, at Margaret and Caroline Streets, is a souvenir shop and museum relating to the Over-Sea Railroad built by Henry Flagler, which operated to Key West between 1912 and 1935.

The building at 1125 Duval Street, now a popular hotel and restaurant with the name slightly changed to "La Te Da," is one of only a few large homes built by a prominent Key West cigar factory owner that remain in the city. Thousands of supporters of Cuban liberation gathered in the street below on May 3, 1883, to listen to Martí's speech.

The balcony of La Te Da at 1125 Duval Street is where José Martí addressed a crowd of thousands on May 3, 1883. The building now hosts a restaurant, hotel, and upstairs cabaret. The modern name was cleverly shortened and adapted from " La Terraza de Martí." The building was originally the home of cigar maker Teodoro Perez.

FORMER FLORIDA FIRST NATIONAL BANK
Front & Duval Streets

This red- and yellow-brick building, with a design resembling some structures in Latin America as well as Spain and elsewhere in Europe of the period, is in the *Neo-Mudéjar* ("new Moorish") style. The building was partially funded by a group of wealthy Cuban cigar manufacturers in Key West and operated for many years as Florida First National Bank. Now a souvenir shop, the building features a corner tower (now shortened from its original height), a carved balcony supported by ornate corbels on the Duval street side, and elaborate capitals on the columns.

This building at the corner of Duval and Front Streets was built as a bank in 1891 by prosperous Cuban-Americans. The alternating brick colors, the corbel-supported balcony, and window details are in the *Neo-Mudéjar* style, a European version of Moorish revival architecture.

CUSTOM HOUSE MUSEUM
281 Front Street

The old Custom House originally housed not only the customs office, but the post office and district courts as well. Today it is a museum and home to the Key West Art and Historical Society. Originally opened in 1891, the building hosted the first inquiry into the explosion of the U.S.S. *Maine* in Havana Harbor. The museum is one of three sites maintained by the Key West Art and Historical Society, along with the East Martello Tower and the Lighthouse museum.

Exhibits in the museum range over the span of Key West history, although the building itself is representative of 1890s municipal architecture, with its Richardsonian Romanesque brick style, so named for Henry Hobson Richardson. Richardson designed numerous municipal and public buildings throughout the United States in the period 1871–1886. He influenced a whole generation of other architects, including Key West resident William Kerr, who followed Richardson's style of imposing masonry or brick structures echoing medieval motifs seen in this building.

Visitors to the museum will see displays related to the era of the Cuban Revolution, the early history of Key West, wrecking, and the city's flourishing as an artists' and writers' colony in later years.

The much-photographed statue in front, showing a dancing couple dressed in 1890s style, was donated by its creator, John Seward Johnson Jr., who also created several other whimsical, sometimes lifelike statues located nearby. These include five dancing nude women, an artist at an easel, and two ladies resting

on a park bench while shopping. Johnson is internationally known for his many painted bronze, surprisingly lifelike tromp l'oeil sculptures. Others are structured of styrofoam and aluminum. Many of them are in public places and much photographed. Johnson's more than 250 sculptures are found around the world, with famous examples in Rockefeller Center, New York; Portland, Oregon; Sydney, Australia; and some sixteen in Carmel, California.

A massive statue by sculptor
J. Seward Johnson provides a
photo op in front of the Key West
Custom House Museum.

SAN CARLOS INSTITUTE
516 Duval Street

One of the most imposing buildings on Duval
Street is the Spanish revival style building
at number 516, built in 1890 to house the
San Carlos Institute. The first home of the San
Carlos Institute in Key West was a small
structure on Anne Street built in 1871. It was
the scene of many meetings of Cuban exiles
plotting the revolution against Spanish rule in
their homeland. The Institute moved from Anne

Street to a larger building on Fleming Street in 1884, but that structure burned in the 1886 fire.

Built in 1890 under the leadership of Key West civic leader Martin Herrera, the new home of the institute reflected the growing affluence of some Cuban entrepreneurs in Key West. However, the building was almost totally destroyed in a hurricane in 1919. With funds and materials from independent Cuba, the rebuilt building became a showplace and museum of Cuban history. Today it is sometimes open to visitors, but funding limitations have restricted the hours. The building contains a large auditorium suitable for concerts, lectures, and performances.

The crest on the front of the structure is a shield with Cuba's coat of arms. Inside the lobby is a copper statue of Father Felix Varela sculpted by Gay Garcia. The José Martí Room gives details on Martí's life and works through pictures and informative labels. Other portraits and their explanatory panels detail the lives of other Cuban revolutionary leaders, including Carlos Manuel de Céspedes and Generals Máximo Gómez and Antonio Maceo Grajales. Ornate hand-painted blue Cuban tiles grace the stairway to the second floor, and the stairway itself is made of marble from Cuba's Isle of Pines.

The first Key West San Carlos Institute was built in 1871 by Cuban-Americans as a meeting place. This building, replacing earlier ones destroyed by fire or storm, houses an elegant museum devoted to Cuban history.

KEY WEST CEMETERY
AND *MAINE* MEMORIAL

In the Key West Cemetery there are numerous reminders of Cuban presence and influence, including a number of gravestones and memorials. The graves of Juana Borrero (poet and painter during the period of the Cuban Revolution), Carlos Recio (Key West Cuban grocer who raised funds for the revolution), Piedad de Ayala (granddaughter of the composer of the Cuban national anthem), and the Gato family plot can be located by picking up the self-guided tour brochure at the sexton's office. That office is at the main gate on Passover Lane off Windsor Street. The brochure includes a map identifying the location of more than fifty other specific graves, all of historic interest.

The *Maine* Memorial in the cemetery is set in a small enclosure the Navy Plot—dedicated to U.S. Navy (and other veteran) graves. The central monument is a bronze statue of a U.S. Navy enlisted man in the uniform of the 1890s, holding an oar. Visitors can spot the location of the Navy Plot and the Maine Memorial by looking for the flagpole to the right of the entrance from Passover Lane/Windsor Street.

On either side of the monument and nearby in the Navy Plot are the graves of 27 sailors who were killed in the explosion of the U.S. battleship *Maine* in Havana harbor on February 15, 1898. (See "Explosion of the USS *Maine*," page 70.) The dead are not identified, but marked as "unknown." The American public, already incensed at Spanish treatment of Cuban civilians and rebels during the uprising that began in 1895, were horrified at the tragedy of the explosion of the *Maine,* which claimed 266 lives of American sailors and officers. Of the 266, 229 were buried at Arlington National Cemetery.

The battle cry of U.S. troops in the Spanish-American War was "Remember the Maine!"

The 1886 Fire Mystery

The fire that destroyed the St. Paul's church in April 1886 has always remained a bit of a mystery. The fire started next to the San Carlos Institute, a gathering place for Cuban exiles who opposed Spanish rule in Cuba, leading to suspicion that it had been started by Spanish agents. The fire started on April 1, 1886. It was nearly extinguished the next morning, when it began again, tearing through the downtown area and destroying cigar factories and cigar workers' homes. Spanish naval ships were waiting off shore to return displaced Cuban workers to Cuba. Most mysteriously of all, a paper printed in Havana reported that Key West had burned down, and the paper was published the day before the fire started.

USS *MAINE* MEMORIAL IN
MALLORY SQUARE

Near the War Memorial in Mallory Square that documents the place of Key West in military history from the early nineteenth century to the present is a small, inconspicuous memorial. This is a sighting turret hood for one of the USS *Maine's* 10-inch guns. The hood would protect a seaman from the enemy's small arms fire while he aimed the large gun.

Since the *Maine* exploded in fairly shallow water in Havana Harbor, many parts of the ship could be salvaged. Literally dozens of pieces of the ship were returned to the United States and mounted as memorials around the country, from Bangor, Maine, to Oakland, California, and points in between. Additionally, plaques were made from metal recovered from the wreck, and they too are memorials.

According to legend, one of the jokes at the Naval Academy about the USS *Maine* was that it was the "longest ship in the U.S. Navy."

In the Key West Cemetery, a statue of a lone sailor with a lifeboat oar overlooks the graves of U.S. sailors who died in the explosion of the USS *Maine* in Havana Harbor, February 15, 1898.

Why? "Because it has its foremast at Annapolis and its mainmast in Arlington Cemetery in Virginia." That answer leaves out the sighting turret, some 1,200 miles from Arlington in Key West!

The remains of some of the victims of the USS *Maine* explosion interred at Key West Cemetery were never identified.

This small plaque in the pavement at the Maine Memorial reminds visitors that the Spanish-American War was fought in the Pacific as well as the Caribbean.

6 Creative Getaway

Flagler's rail line brought tourists to Key West through the 1920s, but the economic downturn of the Great Depression threatened to cut off tourism. The Labor Day hurricane of 1935 that severed the rail line also devastated homes and marinas and resulted in an estimated 408 deaths, mostly in the upper Keys. (See "Labor Day Hurricane," page 72.) One passenger train carrying people fleeing from the storm was entirely washed off the tracks. Some 300 bodies were later cremated at Islamorada, where a crypt and monument commemorate the tragedy.

With the rail line washed out, ferries connected Key West to the mainland, carrying cars, trucks, and buses over the ocean gaps in the road. Direct roadway communication to the city was not established until 1938, after the East Coast Railway ceded the right of way to the state and U.S. Highway 1 was extended by bridges to Key West.

This monument to the hundreds of victims of the 1935 hurricane is found right next to U.S. Highway 1, near mile marker 82 on Islamorada.

Key West in Prohibition

Despite the coming of the railroad and the eventual highway link, Key West fell on hard times. All of the businesses that had once made millionaires in the town had dried up or moved elsewhere. Wrecking had nearly vanished because sailing ships had been largely replaced by steamships that could avoid being blown ashore in most conditions. Sponging had moved to Tarpon Springs; pineapples had been replaced by Cuban and other imports; the turtle soup fad had passed; cigar-making had moved to Tampa, and cigarettes were supplanting cigars by the 1920s. So, even before the Great Depression hit the rest of the country in 1929–1930, Key West saw one of the highest rates of unemployment in the country.

In the period 1920–1933, the Volstead Act prohibited the manufacture, sale, or import of alcoholic beverages, but it did not prohibit their consumption. The Roaring Twenties saw the proliferation of strategies for openly flaunting the law.

While speakeasies and rum-runners flourished through the 1920s and early 1930s in Key West, the high unemployment rate pushed the city towards bankruptcy. Beginning in the late 1920s, writers and artists found refuge in the city, attracted by its low-cost housing, its tropical climate, and its Caribbean cultural flavor.

Key West in Literary History: Hemingway

Ernest Hemingway and several other well-known American writers of the 1920s lived abroad in France or Spain—Gertrude Stein, F. Scott Fitzgerald, and John Dos Passos, among others. Gertrude Stein had coined the phrase "the Lost Generation" to refer to the Paris expatriates, and Hemingway concluded his later novel, *The Sun Also Rises,* with the phrase. In the late 1920s and the 1930s, some of

> ### Hemingway's Wives
>
> *Hemingway met Pauline Pfeiffer in 1925 at a party in Paris, which he attended with his first wife, Hadley Richardson. At the time Pauline was working for Vogue magazine as a writer and assistant editor. Hemingway was living in the community of expatriate American artists and writers who included Cole Porter, Gertrude Stein, Ezra Pound, John Dos Passos, and F. Scott Fitzgerald. Hadley and Pauline became friends, and Pauline began to spend more and more time with the Hemingways, including using her editing skills to critique Ernest's writing. In 1927, Hemingway divorced Hadley Richardson and married Pauline Pfeiffer to whom he remained married during his Key West years. They were divorced in 1940. Hemingway married Martha Gelhorn later in 1940, then Mary Welsh in 1946.*

the expatriate writers returned to the United States, most continuing to reflect the sense of alienation from conservative or "puritan" American values represented by the Volstead Act and Prohibition. Some later settled in art colonies in the United States like Big Sur in California or Greenwich Village in New York City. In effect, they pursued their escape from what they disliked about conventional life in America while still living within the boundaries of the USA. Key West became just such a creative getaway in the period.

Returning to the U.S. from France in 1928, Hemingway and his second wife, Pauline, sailed from Marseilles to Havana, and then took the Peninsular and Occidental shipping line to Key West. When they arrived, Hemingway expected to find a car that Pauline's uncle, Gus Pfieffer, had purchased for him, but the local Ford dealer was still awaiting delivery of the vehicle. Ernest and Pauline Hemingway stayed at 314 Simonton Street—"Casa An-

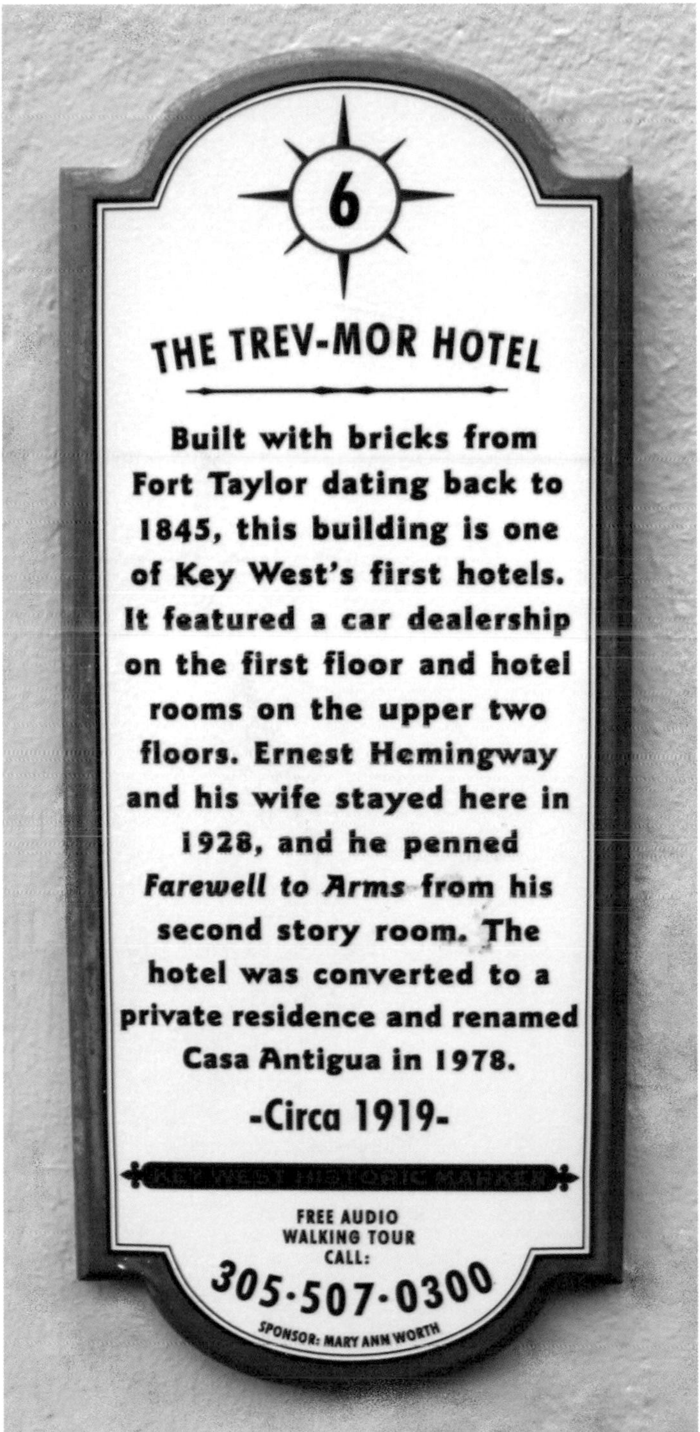

THE TREV-MOR HOTEL

Built with bricks from Fort Taylor dating back to 1845, this building is one of Key West's first hotels. It featured a car dealership on the first floor and hotel rooms on the upper two floors. Ernest Hemingway and his wife stayed here in 1928, and he penned *Farewell to Arms* from his second story room. The hotel was converted to a private residence and renamed Casa Antigua in 1978.

-Circa 1919-

KEY WEST HISTORIC MARKER

FREE AUDIO
WALKING TOUR
CALL:
305·507·0300
SPONSOR: MARY ANN WORTH

This historic marker on the former Trev-Mor Hotel, now Casa Antigua, at 314 Simonton Street documents the first stay of Ernest Hemingway in Key West, 1928–29.

tigua"—which had apartments over the Ford car dealership. It is now a souvenir shop. While there awaiting delivery of the car, Hemingway worked on *A Farewell to Arms,* a novel based on his own experience as an ambulance driver in World War I.

Some may find the name of the current shop on the first floor rather jarring: "Pelican Poop."

Although Hemingway had already published some six books and was well known in Paris and New York, most local Key West folks had never heard of him or his books and accepted him as an interesting fellow who liked to fish. His circle of friends included locals Charles Thompson, who was an avid tarpon fisherman, and Joe Russell, who ran a charter boat and also operated a speakeasy. Hemingway developed nicknames for his friends, and Joe Russell became known as "Sloppy Joe."

Hemingway invited other friends to come to Key West, among them the writers John Dos

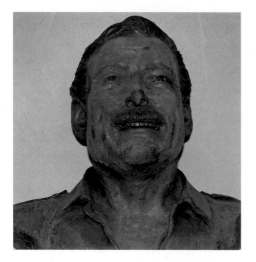

Among the busts at the Sculpture Garden is this one honoring Ernest Hemingway (1899–1961), who made a home in Key West through the 1930s.

Passos and Archibald MacLeish and the artists Henry Strater and Waldo Pierce, all of whom he knew from his time in France. This group, together with other locals and visitors, became well known as "Hemingway's Mob." Pierce painted a portrait of Hemingway that later appeared on the cover of *Time* magazine, as well as pictures of local Key West hangouts, including the dance hall next to Sloppy Joe's bar.

Hemingway visited Key West in the following winters, and in 1931, Gus Pfeiffer offered to buy Ernest and Pauline Hemingway a house to live in while in Key West. The home at 907 Whitehead, built in 1851 by Asa Tift, was in run-down condition, almost a ruin. The house underwent several months of repairs, and after a stay in Spain the couple moved into the home in December 1931. As noisy repairs continued on the house, Hemingway worked in his studio in the backyard on *Death in the Afternoon,* his novel about Spanish bullfighting.

Hemingway was a prolific writer, but only one of his books was set in Key West: *To Have and Have Not* (1937). It featured a fictional character, Harry Morgan, who operated as a liquor, immigrant, and Cuban rebel smuggler from Cuba to Key West. The book was actually written while Hemingway was in Spain during the Spanish Civil War. Later, local Key West fishermen friends formed the basis for the central character in the short novel *The Old Man and the Sea* for which Hemingway won the Nobel Prize in 1954. Details of Hemingway's life in Key West are explored at greater length in Stuart McIver's *Hemingway's Key West* (Pineapple Press, 2012).

Elmer Davis, the popular radio news broadcaster and journalist, came to know and love Key West in the period, seeing it as part of the art colony movement of the era. Davis said, "It was Greenwich Village, Montparnasse, Provincetown—on a little tropical island."

Key West in the New Deal

While Hemingway and his friends enjoyed the freedom of Key West, for the majority of locals the collapse of the economy was devastating. By 1934, the city was bankrupt. Of the city's population of 13,000 (down from 26,000 in 1910), it was estimated that 80 percent were out of work. City fathers asked the state's governor to declare a state of emergency so that the city could be turned over to the federal government for a bail-out.

The Federal Emergency Relief Agency (FERA) made Key West one of its projects, providing funds for construction and cooperating with other federal agencies to try to get Key West back on its feet. Under the leadership of Julius Stone Jr., FERA organized a team of volunteers to clean up buildings in disrepair and to try to convert the town into a tourist attraction. Julius Stone's methods were unorthodox, and some, including Hemingway, criticized him for high-handed and dictatorial methods.

This is one of two New Deal-style murals painted in 1934 by Alfred Crimi inside the Key West Aquarium, capturing the era's respect for manual work.

With the help of city planners, engineers, and federal funds reported at $1 million, Stone worked to get the city in shape. Volunteers collected garbage and trash, dumping it in the ocean. Using federal money and volunteers, Stone replaced outhouses with a modern sewer system. Some 200 small homes were remodeled and rented out. Stone visualized Key West as a tourist destination, and promoted the town as America's only Caribbean island that tourists could drive to. Working to capture the tropical ambience, he encouraged people to go to work in Bermuda shorts in an era when a suit, dress shirt, and tie were proper attire even for store clerks and office workers.

Julius Stone's plan began to work, and by 1940, local unemployment had fallen by two-thirds. The Works Progress Administration funneled more money through the Federal Art Project, which supported professional artists who were out of funds. Among the artists brought to Key West under the WPA were Stanley Wood and Avery Johnson. Later artists included Alfred Crimi, Eric Johan Smith, Adrian Dornbush, Richard Jensen, and Peter Rotier. Their paintings and murals were on display throughout the town. Because they were produced for the government, these works were copyright-free and thus widely reproduced. Under the terms of the Federal Art

The Key West Art Center at 301 Front Street is descended from the New Deal Works Projects Administration (WPA) art center established in 1937.

Project, an artist had to be unemployed, agree not to produce abstract art, and work for a stipend of $24 a week. Across the United States, some 6,000 artists eventually participated in the Federal Art Project. In Key West, the combination of government-fostered renovation under the management of Julius Stone and government-supported art provided a unique mix.

As the reputation of Key West spread, even more artists came to the town with or without federal aid. The WPA helped the city build the Key West Art Center, which soon became the center for lessons, demonstrations, gallery exhibits, and lectures. It was one of almost 100 such centers around the nation. The many works of art representing Key West beaches, homes, lush foliage, and many local characters helped publicize the community and bring visitors, with many reproduced as postcards and posters. The FERA and WPA projects had left a definite mark, and the idea of Key West as a combination art colony and tourist destination had been firmly planted. The Key West Art Center, which opened in 1960, claims descent from the WPA center at the original location at 301 Front Street.

During stays in Spain and Cuba, Hemingway grew fond of cats. Those inhabiting the Hemingway House today are descendents of the polydactyl or six-toed cats he owned here.

SITES

HEMINGWAY HOUSE

Built in 1850–1851, and in disrepair when purchased for Hemingway by his wealthy uncle-in-law Gus Pfeiffer, the house at 907 Whitehead Street is now open to visitors for a charge, payable at the front gate to the property. Guided or self-guided tours are available, with highlights including the high-ceilinged interior, the bookshop (featuring, of course, Hemingway books), the swimming pool (the first in Key West), and the many six-toed cats, descended from those owned by Hemingway.

Guides like to tell the story of the cat watering trough in the backyard, once the urinal at Sloppy Joe's Bar and rescued by Hemingway when it was torn out. Hemingway's original studio, upstairs in a separate building in the back, is not currently open to visitors.

The building not only commemorates the life of Hemingway, but it helps to physically document the place of Key West in American literary history, accounting for its popularity as a tourist destination. It is on the must-see list of most visitors.

The Hemingway House at 907 Whitehead Street was built in 1851 by Asa Tift and purchased for Hemingway in 1931 by his wife's uncle.

KEY WEST AQUARIUM
1 Whitehead Street

The Key West Aquarium was first planned by Dr. Robert O. Van Deusen, then director of the Fairmount Park Aquarium in Philadelphia, which operated from 1911 to 1962 as one of the four largest aquariums in the world in its time. Construction of the Key West Aquarium began in 1933 as part of the Works Progress Administration plans for rejuvenating the city, providing jobs as well as a future attraction. The aquarium opened on February 18, 1935.

Following ideas of Van Deusen, the aquarium used an open-air plan, allowing natural sunlight to shine into the concrete tanks holding marine displays, which were to focus on local sea-life. Van Deusen attended the opening and proclaimed two important functions of the new facility: It would serve as a valuable marine biology institution, setting precedents for more such around the world; and it would aid in the birth of Key West as a tourist destination. However, just a few months after opening, the washout of the railway suddenly cut off the trickle of tourists. After a period of decline, the federal government leased the aquarium to the navy in 1943 for use as a rifle range by sailors and other military personnel stationed in and near Key West.

In 1946, after the end of World War II, the

The Key West Aquarium was built in 1933–35 with New Deal funding as a tourist attraction to help revive the local economy.

aquarium was turned over to the City of Key West for restoration. By the 1960s, the idea of a sunlit, open-air aquarium was dated, and a roof was added with more modern lighting for the interior tanks. Today the aquarium remains a popular attraction, with a focus on local sea creatures and ecological preservation, blending a small marine display with the historic feature of a Depression-era effort to boost the local economy.

Popular attractions now include shark, barracuda, and turtle feedings in outdoor tanks, and a touch tank that allows children to literally have a hands-on experience with sea stars, sea cucumbers, and other sea life that don't bite. The aquarium features a wide variety of fish, including moray eels, grouper, tarpon, parrotfish, and others from nearby waters. The aquarium works with other Florida marine institutions in stranded turtle rescue, and several injured turtles remain in its collection.

THE SPEAKEASY INN
1117 Duval Street

The Speakeasy Inn operates today as a small hotel with a colorful bar and an even more colorful history. The home of Raul Vasquez (1890–1957), a Tampa-born cigar worker at the Gato Cigar Factory, it became known as a popular watering hole and gambling resort during Prohibition. According to local legend, Vasquez ordered the specially cut balcony woodwork from Cuba. If you look closely at the pattern made by the cutouts, you can recognize whiskey and wine bottles as well as smaller spades, hearts, clubs, and diamonds, suggesting a casino. While it would have been too obvious during Prohibition to post a "speakeasy" sign, the wooden balcony served as a not-so-subtle reminder of the libations and entertainments available within.

Raul Vasquez became well known for operating a small boat running back and forth to Cuba for liquor supplies. Arrested by Prohibition agents, he was incarcerated in the local jail, where the jailors conveniently released him during the day to conduct his business; he would return faithfully at night. One legend has it that the guard provided Vasquez with a key to the jail so he could return to his cell when the guard had gone off duty!

According to local lore, this carved balustrade at the Speakeasy Inn once signified the entertainments within, with its cutouts in the shape of bottles and playing card pips or symbols.

BIRTHPLACE OF PAN AM

At the intersection of Caroline and Whitehead Streets is a modest white building, now part of "The Southernmost Brewery." Briefly in the 1920s, this building was the headquarters of Pan American Airways, which had its start in Key West and would grow to become the leading U.S. passenger airline in the two following decades.

The first flight was in a seaplane Pan Am founder and entrepreneur Juan Trippe rented from a company that was having it delivered to the Dominican Republic. Regular passenger service began on January 16, 1928, flying between Key West and Havana.

In 1928, Trippe moved the headquarters to a new terminal in Miami, on the waterfront where passengers could await their flight aboard Pan Am "clippers"—large seaplanes—that would dock right below the observation-restaurant. The terminal building there is now Miami City Hall.

Juan Trippe pioneered the ideas of jet-powered passenger air travel as well as "tourist"-level accommodations. In 1958, the first Pan Am jet flight from New York to Paris ushered in the age of jet travel. It all had its beginning in Key West in 1927.

CAPTAIN TONY'S SALOON
428 Greene Street

The building built in the 1850s that housed Captain Tony's Saloon during the 1930s already had a long and colorful history, having served as an icehouse, a morgue, a telegraph station, a bordello, and a speakeasy.

In the early 1930s, Joe Russell, who owned a charter boat business, bought the speakeasy and then, with the end of Prohibition in 1933, opened the saloon legally as Sloppy Joe's Bar. From 1933 to 1938, the bar was one of Hemingway's favorite hangouts. Joe Russell had a dispute with the landlord over rent,

Captain Tony's Saloon was the site of the original Sloppy Joe's, frequented by Ernest Hemingway and his friends in the early 1930s.

and suddenly moved out to the present location of Sloppy Joe's on Duval Street. So both buildings have a legitimate claim to the Sloppy Joe heritage.

After Joe Russell moved his bar to Duval Street, the building at 428 Greene Street became the Duval Club, offering gay parties. The navy soon placed the bar off limits. The building acquired its present name in 1958 when Captain Tony Terracino bought the building, operating it as Captain Tony's until 1989. Subsequent proprietors have kept the name.

Proprietors have retained many mementos of past patrons from the bar's long history. ID cards, autographed bras, signed dollar bills, and barstools with names of prior visitors, including Hemingway, Truman, John F. Kennedy, and Jimmy Buffet, add to the atmosphere. Among the ghost stories associated with the building is that of the "Lady in Gray," reputedly the spirit of a woman who was hanged for the crime of murdering her husband from the tree that still stands inside the bar.

Sloppy Joe's Saloon, on the corner of Duval and Greene Streets, has been at this location since 1937.

7 World War II and the Post-War Years

Key West played an important part in the history of World War II, especially in the campaign to stop German submarine operations off the Florida coast. As early as January 1942, German long-range submarines began sinking U.S. ships, particularly oil tankers, in nearby waters. German subs attacked and sank dozens of tankers, along with cargo ships carrying coffee, minerals, sugar, and other products of the Americas bound for Britain. German submarine attacks reached a peak in May 1942, when four U-boats sank more than forty ships off the Florida coast.

Operating out of Key West, U.S. Army Air Force and Navy patrol craft and destroyers searched for German U-boats in the Straits of Florida, off the Bahamas and Cuba, and out into the Atlantic. Aircraft from the Key West Naval Air Station flew regular patrols, as did PBY flying boats operating out of the Key West Naval Base, hunting for the German submarines, which could only operate underwater for a few hours at a time before resurfacing to recharge their batteries by running on diesel power.

As a method of protecting tankers and freighters from submarine attack, ships were routed in convoys, that is, groups of cargo-carrying ships protected by destroyers or destroyer escorts. One such convoy assembled and operated from Key West in July and August 1942, running to and from Curaçao and Aruba by way of Trinidad. Another convoy system operated after August 1942 between Key West and New York. Although some ships were lost to submarine attack when in convoy, the losses were greatly reduced with the convoy system. When a ship in a convoy was torpedoed by a submarine, other ships would rescue most or all of the sailors, while the protecting destroyers could chase down and drive off or sink the enemy submarine.

Facilities

The U.S. Navy activated the Naval Base Key West at Trumbo Point in November 1939. Trumbo Point was a piece of landfill that had been constructed originally by Flagler's company for the terminus of the Florida East Coast rail line and the shipping point for ferries to Cuba. Today Trumbo Point houses several naval and other defense facilities and has vacation rental units available to active and retired military personnel.

The facility was redesignated Naval Air Station Key West by December 1940. With three submarines and four destroyers based there, the navy also ran a sonar school, one of three such schools in the country. Other aircraft operating out of the base included OS2U Kingfishers (catapult-launched float planes) and PBM Mariners (patrol flying boat bombers). The naval base also hosted a squadron of Catalina flying boats.

Meacham Field, today's Key West International Airport, was converted to an army air field immediately after the Japanese attack on Pearl Harbor. Army antisubmarine aircraft and P-40 Warhawk fighters flew out from Meacham. In March of 1945 the various naval facilities on Key West became consolidated as Naval Air

Station Key West and Meacham Field returned to civilian control. The number of navy, marine, army, and coast guard personnel and their dependents in Key West climbed to a peak of more than 15,000 in 1945. Into the post-war years, the continued presence of the military in Key West provided one of the main sources of income for the town's retail businesses.

Harry S. Truman's "Little White House"

President Harry Truman began visiting Key West in November 1946, setting up a "Little White House." Altogether he stayed in Key West 175 days, spending eleven working vacations here during his seven-year presidency. Truman enjoyed Key West so much that after he retired from office, he made five more visits over the period 1957–1969, staying at a private home in town rather than at the Little White House. Today the Truman Little White House is one the most popular

Harry S. Truman

When President Franklin D. Roosevelt died on April 12, 1945, Vice President Harry S. Truman was sworn in as president. Roosevelt had been elected four times, in 1932, 1936, 1940, and 1944. Truman was Roosevelt's third vice president and had previously served as U.S. senator from Missouri. In the Senate he had gained recognition for heading a congressional investigation into excessive profits in the war industries. Although Roosevelt had kept Truman only partly informed (he learned of the Manhattan Project that built the atomic bomb only after taking office), Truman turned out to be a popular and effective president. He was re-elected in 1948 for a full term as president. Truman's down-to-earth style was a good match for Key West.

historic sites in the town—the only presidential residence in Florida—and serving as a reminder of Truman and his era.

The World War II years had brought brief wartime prosperity to Key West, but after the war, the economy of the town fell off, with many buildings abandoned and falling into disrepair. A number of long-time resident families, some descended from the pre-Civil War generation pioneers, continued to live in and keep up some of the old mansions. Charter boats still attracted sports fishermen, and President Truman himself often went out on the charters. Key West remained a departure and arrival point for ferries to and from Cuba up through 1959, and the military remained a presence, with the bi-monthly federal paychecks and the shopping of military families helping to prop up the retail sector. However, in the post-World War II era of the late 1940s to the 1960s, other businesses that had once brought prosperity to the town had all declined as technologies and consumer tastes changed, or they had moved on to more profitable locales.

In the midst of the economic hard times, temporary relief came with a new fishing industry: shrimping.

Pink Gold

In 1950, new shrimp trawling areas were found off the Dry Tortugas by a fisherman, John Salvadore. Examining a haul from his seines near dusk, he found more shrimp than he expected. He lowered the trawls for a second run and pulled in even more.

John Salvadore was the son of Sallecito Salvadore, a Sicilian immigrant who settled in Amelia Island, Florida, where he had pioneered shrimping in the early 1900s. Soon after John Salvadore's discovery of shrimp beds in the Dry Tortugas, the new industry brought new

The shrimp boat *Captain G.C.II*, built in 1996, is a lonely reminder of the several hundred shrimpers that once operated out of Key West and Stock Island.

fortunes to Key West and Stock Island. Because the local shrimp were pink, the harvests became known as "pink gold." By 1956, some 300 shrimp trawlers, some relocated from ports elsewhere in the Gulf, operated out of Key West, docking in the historic Bight area at the foot of Margaret Street.

Sports fishermen soon learned that one way to ensure a good catch of blackfin tuna and other large fish was to follow a shrimper. When the shrimp fishermen cleaned the "trash" fish out of their nets and tossed the unwanted catch overboard, tuna, bonita, king fish, sharks, and other large fish came to feed on the discards. Sports fishermen were guaranteed a good catch of some kind from the feeding frenzy as they trailed in the wake of free bait.

However, the practice of scooping up vast amounts "trash" fish as well as shrimp raised concerns about overfishing and damage to the ecosystem. Then, through the 1980s, as shrimp-farming proliferated through the Far East and Central and South America, the low price of farm-raised shrimp undercut the trawling business, not only in Key West, but in ports in Louisiana, Mississippi, and Alabama as well. Despite the fact that imported farm-raised shrimp often were loaded with chemicals and dyes, restaurants and groceries across the United States met the growing national demand for shrimp with the imported farm-raised shrimp rather than fresh-caught shrimp from Gulf waters. A few restaurants in Key West and Stock Island continued to buy locally caught shrimp, but by the 2010s, only three shrimp trawlers continued to operate locally. Like many other thriving American enterprises of the twentieth century, Key West shrimp trawling was put out of business by a combination of environmental regulation and foreign competition.

During the Cuban Missile Crisis of 1962, the army set up four HAWK missile sites to protect Key West airfields. This and other nearby radar towers from one of the emplacements north of Key West International Airport are off-the-beaten-track twentieth century ruins.

Key West in the Cold War:
The HAWK Missiles

The "hottest" crisis of the more than 40-year-long Cold War between the United States and the Soviet Union came in October 1962 with the Cuban Missile Crisis, which had an immediate impact on Key West. On October 22, President Kennedy, in a tense television broadcast, announced to a stunned American audience that the Soviet Union was setting up missile sites on Cuba. The medium-range missiles could target most cities in the United States, and Kennedy called the sites "a deliberately provocative" action.

In response, President Kennedy ordered a naval blockade of Cuba; meanwhile, nuclear-armed B-52 aircraft stayed aloft in order to provide an immediate retaliatory nuclear strike on the Soviet Union if needed. On October 27, a Soviet-made anti-aircraft missile shot down an American U-2 surveillance plane over Cuba.

As part of the raised defenses of the United States, Kennedy ordered the deployment of anti-aircraft missiles in Florida, including four installations in and around Key West. HAWK ("Homing All the Way Killer") missiles arrived in town and were installed on October 26, at the height of the crisis. At first, one such missile battery was set up on Smathers Beach, just south of the East Martello Tower, in plain sight of locals walking by on South Roosevelt Boulevard. Later, four additional installations were set up, each with radar towers and earthen embankments around the missile sites. They were located to protect the airport, the base at Boca Chica, and the Naval Air Station.

Although the missile crisis blew over when Soviet Premier Nikita Khrushchev agreed on October 28 to remove the missiles from Cuba, the HAWK anti-aircraft missile sites in Key West remained active until 1979. Today, all of the sites have been long abandoned, and no markers or other indications of their existence have been posted. However, five of the radar towers remaining from "Bravo Site" can be viewed from the end of Government Road (reached from Hagler Avenue), north of Key West International Airport, while other radar towers at the "Charlie Site" near the Boca Chica air base can be seen from Boundary Lane or Boca Chica Road on Geiger Key. These towers once housed radar units that would be able to illuminate incoming aircraft or target them for the anti-aircraft HAWK missiles.

Mariel Boatlift: April 1980–September 1980

The Mariel boatlift of refugees from Cuba began in early 1980 following episodes when thousands of Cubans sought political asylum in the Peruvian Embassy in Havana. Faced with the embarrassing crisis, Castro announced that anyone wishing to leave Cuba could do so from the port of Mariel, as long as they provided their own transportation. As word of the open port spread, hundreds of small craft from Florida sailed for Mariel to pick up the refugees, most of the boats financed by Cubans already resident in the United States.

On April 24, 1980, an estimated one thousand boats were seen being hauled by trailer along U.S. Route 1 towards Key West. Boats lined up in Key West to launch, and at one point Cuban authorities announced that there were more than 1,700 boats waiting to pick up refugees in Mariel. After some disasters at sea, and many rescues by the U.S. Coast Guard and navy ships, the Cuban government ended the exodus in September 1980. Altogether about 125,000 refugees fled Cuba before Castro ordered the port closed.

Although many refugees returned through Key West, the U.S. government set up relocation camps in Ft. Chaffee, Arkansas, Ft. McCoy, Wisconsin, and Ft. Indiantown Gap, Pennsylvania. Altogether, an estimated 80,000 of the refugees settled in the Miami area.

No historic sites in Key West are devoted to the boatlift, but information about the Mariel refugees and some of the improvised boats used then and at other times can be found at the Custom House Museum, in a display at the Martello East Tower, and at the Key West Tropical Forest and Botanical Garden.

Conch Republic

Throughout Key West, visitors will find flags of the "Conch Republic," including a prominent mural at the airport. The flags have become the unofficial emblem of the town since the "secession" of Key West from the United States on April 23, 1982. The event came in response to a U.S. Border Patrol blockade set up on U.S. Highway 1 at Florida City. Residents coming from the Florida Keys were asked to show identification and were outraged at the resulting delays. Being asked to prove American citizenship before driving onto the mainland seemed an insult.

After Key West Mayor Dennis Wardlow sought a federal injunction to stop the blockade,

The Conch Republic flag is found throughout Key West, a semi-serious reminder that Key West is a unique place since "Independence" was declared in 1982.

he announced to reporters that the Florida Keys would secede from the United States. The next day, Wardlow read the proclamation of secession in Mallory Square. To cap off the ceremony, the mayor broke a loaf of Cuban bread over the head of a man dressed as a U.S. sailor. Then, as "prime minister," Wardlow surrendered to the admiral in command of the Key West navy base, then demanded $1 billion in foreign aid.

Since then, a small group of Conch Republic advocates have continued to make news, sometimes seeking foreign recognition, and getting Monroe County resolutions supporting the "independence" of the Florida Keys. Every year in April there is an anniversary celebration of Conch Republic Independence. Among mementos of the independence are not only the flags (showing the date 1828, when Key West was first set up as municipality), but also "Conch Republic Passports" obtainable online. Although persisting as a long-running joke, the Conch Republic story does capture some of the sense of difference in the Florida Keys and in Key West in particular, and the persistence of the flags, emblems, and sentiment reflects Key West's self-identification as a unique destination.

SITES

TRUMAN WHITE HOUSE
111 Front Street

When Truman visited Key West during his presidency, he stayed in this large white home in the navy compound. Built in 1880 on what was then the waterfront, the building was originally a duplex, known as Quarters A and Quarters B, for the commandant of the navy base and the paymaster. When the naval base harbor was dredged out in 1909 to accommodate larger ships, the shallow water in front of Quarters A and B was filled in; in 1911, the building was converted into a single-family home.

Truman was not the first president to stay in the residence, nor the last. In December 1912, President William Howard Taft stayed there. After Truman revived the tradition, Dwight Eisenhower, John F. Kennedy, Lyndon B. Johnson, Jimmy Carter, and Bill Clinton all spent working vacations there or visited in retirement.

Truman first stayed in the home in 1946, when his doctor recommended a warmer climate and a vacation to break a persistent cold brought on by overwork and stress. Today the building

is outfitted with mementos and furnishings related to the Truman era. Tour docents point out the table where Truman played poker with his friends, the desk where he made decisions, and the bedrooms where he, his wife Bess, and their daughter Margaret stayed.

USCGC *INGHAM*

At the foot of Southard Street, you will find the U.S. Coast Guard Cutter *Ingham* moored as a floating museum, open to visitors. The *Ingham* represents the other six nearly identical ships that participated in World War II's Battle of the Atlantic.

President Harry S. Truman spent 175 days here during eleven visits between 1946 and 1953.

Even before the United States entered World War II, the ship played an important role, serving as a member of the "Neutrality Patrol." Under this arrangement, U.S. Navy and Coast Guard ships cruised the seas between North America and Iceland, reporting the presence of German U-boats.

After the United States joined the war in December 1941, *Ingham,* along with the six

U.S. Coast Guard Cutter *Ingham* is now a floating museum telling the story of the ship's 54-year service, including World War II duty as a convoy escort.

other coast guard cutters of the same class, became a crucial part of the escort system for convoys of ships crossing the Atlantic carrying cargo to the Allies. Altogether *Ingham* escorted seventeen convoys across the Atlantic, and the cutter was the last U.S. warship to sink a German U-boat during the war, sinking U-626 on December 15, 1942.

Following World War II, *Ingham* went on more typical coast guard duties, including search and rescue and weather patrol. In 1968–1969, *Ingham* served off Vietnam, and later participated in the Mariel boatlift of refugees fleeing from Cuba in 1980, escorting Cuban refugee ships into Key West. *Ingham* was decommissioned May 27, 1988. When retired, the cutter was the oldest commissioned warship in the United States, having served for fifty-four years.

The ship was put on display in Key West and is registered as a National Historic Landmark. The setting near the Truman Little White House and the Navy Yard is appropriate given the ship's long and much-decorated career, especially in World War II, and its connection with Key West in the rescue of Cuban refugees.

MARGARET-TRUMAN LAUNDERETTE

When a launderette opened in 1955 on the corner of Margaret Street and Truman Avenue, it was named, appropriately enough, the Margaret-Truman Launderette. When reporters asked Margaret Truman if she minded, she laughed and said it was fine. The owners offered to do her laundry for free if she would revisit Key West, but she admitted in 1957 that she had no plans for a visit to the city.

The naming of the Margaret Truman Launderette reflects a bit of Key West humor.

Margaret Truman had just published her first book, *Souvenir,* her own life story. She later went on to become a popular author of some twenty-five murder mysteries as well as ten nonfiction works.

When the proprietors were asked by a reporter from the *Deseret News* (March 20, 1957) if they had gotten permission to name the launderette after the president's daughter, they pointed out that it was not necessary. After all, the name was hyphenated, and it legitimately described the address of the shop at the corner of the Margaret Street and Truman Avenue. "Even if she had objected, which everybody knew she wouldn't, because she's such a sweet girl," said the owners, Mr. and Mrs. Fred Haas, "there would have been no legal difficulties." While Truman Avenue had been

named for her father, Margaret Street was named for Margaret Whitehead, a sister of pioneer John Whitehead. More than sixty-five years after it first opened, the launderette remains in business under the same name.

TRUMAN ANNEX

After the death of Harry Truman in December 1972, the land of the naval station surrounding the commandant's quarters (Truman's Little White House) was designated the "Truman Annex" in 1973. In March 1974, the Key West Naval Station was disestablished, and the land fell into disuse until 1986, when it was purchased by a developer from Maine, Pritam Singh. While developing the property as an upscale neighborhood of homes and condominiums, Singh donated the Truman Little

The homes in the Truman Annex provide a secluded haven from the bustle of downtown Key West.

White House itself to the State of Florida in January 1987, and it is operated by a private firm under contract with the state.

The elegant and secluded Annex contains a number of structures reflecting the long naval history of Key West, although they have not been set up as historic attractions. For example, the Marine Hospital, first constructed in 1844 at 405 Emma Street at the corner of Emma and Fleming Street, is now a condominium apartment building.

The ambience of the secluded Truman Annex conveys the feeling of Key West officers' quarters in the mid-twentieth century. During World War II and through the post-war years, the Naval Station was an active base, with controlled access through the gates like those now found at the open walking entrance at Whitehead and Caroline Street.

FLORIDA KEYS HISTORIC WAR MEMORIAL, MALLORY SQUARE

In Mallory Square, an unusual war memorial honors not only those from Key West who served in World War II, but has markers and descriptions of the role of Key West in eight other conflicts. Arranged in a semicircle, the nine monuments are in chronological order from left to right: the Anti-Piracy Campaign that began in 1823, the Second Seminole War of the 1830s, the Civil War (1861–1865), the Spanish-American War (1898), World War I (1917–1918), World War II (1941–1945), the Cuban Missile Crisis (1962), the Cold War (1948–1988), and the War on Drugs into the present. A nearby marker lists the names of military personnel from the Florida Keys who lost their lives in the service.

Even though it is a memorial to all the wars in which Key West played a part, the memorial has a special relationship to the post-World War II era. In 2003 at the unveiling of the multi-war memorial, Jack King, the chairman of the committee that raised funds for the memorial, noted that the military presence in Key West provided a source of income for many local businesspeople in the years following World War II, including his own family. The committee sought to memorialize the military's link to Key West, honoring the part that the military played in the economic and cultural survival of the city through the tough times of the 1950s and 1960s.

The War Memorial in Mallory Square was established in recognition of the role the military in Key West history since the 1820s, from the anti-piracy campaign to the Cuban missile crisis and the war on drugs.

8   Rebirth as a Destination

In recent years, Key West has flourished as a combination retirement community, getaway destination, and tourist attraction. One factor was the nationwide revival of interest in historic preservation, a movement spurred on in part by the nation's bicentennial in 1976. Local residents, well aware of the unique history of Key West and its architecture, worked to preserve and restore individual buildings even prior to 1976.

However, a more fundamental historic development accounted for the attraction of Key West as a destination city. By the mid-1960s, the growing counterculture movement of the baby-boom generation had begun to flower. Responding to icons of rebellion and rejection of old-fashioned morality, baby boomers found an enduring attraction in the lifestyle and writings of Ernest Hemingway as well as several other writers like John Dos Passos, Archibald MacLeish, and Wallace Stevens. In the 1930s and 1940s these writers had found temporary or long term escape in Key West, and their various definitions of "escape" appealed to those "born after the bomb and before the pill" (1945–1960)—the baby boomers.

Around the United States, some of the art colonies and writer retreats of the 1920s and earlier decades, such as Carmel, California, and Fire Island, New York, became "gentrified" in later generations, as the panache and fame attached to the locales made them attractive to people of wealth. Through a similar process, Key West would retain some of its reputation

At the intersection of White Street and Atlantic Boulevard, on the beach side, this memorial commemorates the loss of more than 1,000 Key West residents to AIDS; their names are inscribed in black marble pavement.

At the corner of Fleming and Whitehead Street is Mile Marker 0 on U.S. Highway 1, a popular spot for snapshots and selfies. Highway 1 was opened in 1938, three years after a major hurricane destroyed the Florida East Coast Railway link to Key West.

as an escape—at once climbing in real estate values but still holding on to its attraction as a getaway for aspiring writers and artists.

In America in the early twenty-first century the counterculture gradually became part of the mainstream. In Key West, the spirit of escape from traditional, conventional values, which had attracted the writers and artists of the 1930s and 1940s, thrived in later decades and into the present. Across the United States in the twenty-first century, state after state enacted laws legalizing gay marriage and relaxing restrictions on the sale of marijuana. Such changes captured the quiet consummation of the baby boom generation rebellion of the 1960s and 1970s. Key West, with its flamboyant party atmosphere, came to represent a destination where some of the aspects of that rebellion, usually carried on privately in other places, could be demonstrated a little more publicly. At the same time, real estate values climbed.

Tourism

By the 1990s and the first decade of the twenty-first century, Key West had come to rival other Florida destinations, as anticipated in the 1930s by the New Deal's local administrator, Julius Stone Jr. With its admirable deep-water port, the city became a regular stop for cruise ships, bringing between 700,000 and 1,000,000 day-visit tourists a year by the early 2000s. In addition, the many hotels, guesthouse vacation rentals, and B&Bs offered accommodations to tens of thousands more who drove by way of the 110-mile over-the-sea highway or flew into Key West International Airport.

Cruise Ships

Eight to ten cruises ships dock in Key West nearly every week, some right next to Mallory Square and others at Pier B at the foot of Front Street or at the Outer Mole at 33 Quay Street. Almost all of the ships stay only one day, with shore time for visitors limited to a few hours, leading to thousands of tourists ashore in the city during the late morning and early afternoon nearly every day. In the winter months of January and February, there are very few days when there are no cruise ships docked at Key West. With many cruise ships departing from Port Canaveral, Fort Lauderdale, or Miami and cruising through the Straits of Florida on their way to destinations in the Caribbean, Key West is a natural and convenient stop.

Cruise stops included ships from U.S-based Carnival, Disney, Regent, and Prestige/Oceania cruise lines, the British-owned Royal Caribbean and Hapag-Lloyd lines, the Netherlands-owned Holland America line, the Italian-owned Costa Crociere and Silversea lines, and the Norwegian Cruise Line.

Cruise ships like this dock just off Mallory Square and at two other locations, bringing nearly a million visitors to Key West annually.

Free-ranging hens and roosters, said to be descended from the Cubalaya cock-fighting breed, strut around Mallory Square.

The wrecking business, the naval presence, the challenge of bringing a railway, all left their mark. The rise and fall of businesses, from pineapples through sponges and turtle soup, cigar-making and speakeasies, made for more rich historic sites, as did the influx of writers and artists in the 1930s and 1940s.

New enterprises sought to profit from the influx of visitors and their varied interests, with many new attractions that had little or no reference to the place of Key West in history. Such businesses include the usual souvenir and T-shirt shops; golf cart, bicycle, and motor scooter rentals; and a wide variety of action-adventure activities such as ski-boat rentals, deep-sea fishing, snorkeling, windsurfing, and waterskiing.

In the twenty-first century, many businesses have attempted (and some have succeeded very well) in earning revenue from the flow of tourists through the town every year. Some of the attractions, as shown in this volume, are closely tied to the place of Key West in local, regional, or broader national and world history.

Thousands gather nightly to view the spectacular sunsets from Mallory Square.

KEY WEST GHOST STORIES

For fans of the paranormal, Key West holds out a number of interesting ghost stories. In addition to the tale of Robert, the Haunted Doll, on display at the East Martello Tower, many of the guesthouses and historic attractions of Key West have ghost tales attached. At the Lighthouse, visitors have spotted an apparition climbing the stairs. At the main Key West Cemetery as well as the small cemetery associated with St. Paul's Church mysterious figures have been seen wandering at night. Captain Geiger's spirit has been reported on the balcony of the Audubon House. If staying at Chelsea House, Curry Mansion Inn, La Concha Hotel, Banyan Resort, or Eaton Lodge, visitors might ask about spirits said to haunt certain rooms and unexplained noises in the night. These and other tales are recounted on organized ghost tours.

Guided tours on these trains save a lot of walking.

Rental scooters and bicycles are a favorite option with visitors for getting around Key West.

Some of these attractions reflect the present-day popularity of strenuous and adventurous outdoor activities. Others capture aspects of history, with tour-train rides and ghost tours. Many, such as the daily sunset-hour street entertainments on Mallory Square, are simply there to benefit from the flow of dollars.

Those with an appreciation for historic American home architecture find that venturing off the busy main Duval Street onto the quiet back streets is very rewarding. The byways are rich with characteristic Key West homes and mansions as well as small cottages, some of which are restored cigar-worker houses of the 1880s and 1890s. A listing of the more notable historic homes is found in the appendix to this volume.

Several of today's modern tourist attraction sites reflect broader historic developments of the contemporary era.

KEY WEST BUTTERFLY AND NATURE CONSERVATORY
1316 Duval Street

Opened in 2003, the Key West Butterfly and Nature Conservatory has become a major attraction, reflecting the modern era's fascination with the natural environment, conservation, and the psychic restorative effect of communing with nature. The name "Conservatory" captures the emphasis on conserving natural phenomena rather than simply exploiting or displaying nature.

With a Victorian facade and 2,000-square-foot plexiglass enclosure, the conservatory is the host to more than fifty species of butterflies and moths, free to flit about in an 85-degree setting. Quiet background music, muted bird cries, and a tropical garden with trickling

One of hundreds of butterflies at the Butterfly Museum and Nature Conservatory. The Key West Butterfly and Nature Conservatory offers a restful retreat for visitors, with dozens of different species of butterflies in a setting of waterfalls, ponds, and lush tropical foliage.

The Key West Tropical Forest and Botanical Garden, just across the bridge onto Stock Island, is an eleven-acre "frost-free" preserve featuring rare birds and dozens of species of tropical plants.

waterways provide a quiet refuge from the more frenetic entertainments of lower Duval Street. Visitors vie for positions to photograph the many beautiful insects as they alight on flowers or feed on the bananas and other fruit laid out in dishes. Benches and gazebos provide spots to linger. It is reputedly good luck if a butterfly lands on you. Tourists are advised to take their time, take photos, and not hurry through without taking advantage of the opportunity to enjoy the beauty and peaceful atmosphere.

KEY WEST TROPICAL FOREST AND BOTANICAL GARDEN
5210 College Road

The Key West Tropical Forest and Botanical Garden was originally set up by the New Deal Federal Emergency Relief Administration (FERA) as part of the 1930s effort to convert

Key West into a tourist attraction. Some eighty species of trees were planted on a plot that originally spread over fifty-five acres. It is the only "frost-free" botanical garden in the contiguous forty-eight United States.

After some years of neglect, the garden has been operated since 1988 by the Key West Botanical Garden Society. Greatly reduced from its original size, now at eleven acres, the garden hosts several attractions. In addition to a small sculpture display, visitors get the opportunity to spot more than fifty species of birds and more than two dozen species of butterflies. A garden guide describes eight self-guided walking tours, two wetland habitats, and two separate butterfly gardens. Among birds spotted in the garden is the rare white-crowned pigeon, depicted by Audubon on

his 1832 visit. Today, the garden is one of the island's less flashy but interesting tourist attractions, continuing to draw visitors, especially those interested in the tropical environment, nature, ecology, and butterfly and bird life.

MARGARITAVILLE
500 Duval Street

Perhaps the laid-back sentiment of Key West is captured best by the lyrics of Jimmy Buffet's "Margaritaville" with its haunting refrain, "Wasted away again in Margaritaville."

Now a worldwide chain of restaurants, the original Margaritaville was established by Jimmy Buffet in 1985. With his hit record by the same name, first performed and recorded in 1977, Jimmy Buffet successfully captured the unique lifestyle of Key West that resulted from the island's many cultural strands as well as from the surge of tourists that began arriving in Key West in the 1970s.

Buffet, a modest genius, became known not only for his unique and offbeat music, but for writing novels and short stories. He built a chain of restaurants and other enterprises reflecting and capturing the Key West ethos. His approach has been wildly successful, with businesses based on the Margaritaville and related themes including, by 2015, some twenty-four restau-

Jimmy Buffet's original Magaritaville Cafe at 500 Duval Street catches the laid-back ambience that its founder made famous.

Guest Houses and B&Bs

There are more than forty inns, guesthouses, and bed-and-breakfasts in Key West, some in restored and renovated historic homes. Among the historic homes converted for visitors are the Eduardo H. Gato House at 1327 Duval Street; the Southernmost House at 1400 Duval Street; the Avalon Guest House (1895) at 1317 Duval Street; the Blue Parrot Inn (1884) at 916 Elizabeth Street; and the Curry Mansion Inn at 501 Caroline. The Curry Mansion was begun in 1855 by William Curry, a wrecker from the Bahamas who became one of the first millionaires in Florida. The building was completed by William's son, Milton Curry, in 1899. Some of the furniture in the parlor dates back to the 1890s.

rants, twenty-four stores, and a hotel, with more planned. The locations range throughout the United States (mostly in the South), the Caribbean, Latin America, Australia, and Canada. The original Margaritaville restaurant at 500 Duval Street is a must-see for many visitors hoping to catch the flavor of Key West.

pipe junction painted to resemble a channel marker buoy. The buoy attracts thousands eager to get a picture posing by the buoy to show friends and relatives back home that they have reached the point. A picture from the Southernmost Buoy can be a fitting culmination for any trip to Key West.

SOUTHERNMOST POINT BUOY

Located on the corner of Whitehead Street and South Street, this marker is one of the most popular free tourist stops in Key West. Put up in 1983 to replace a sign that had been repeatedly stolen, the marker is not really a buoy, but is a surplus concrete sewer

The Southernmost Point Buoy, at the corner of South and Whitehead Streets, remains one of the most popular photo ops on the island.

Key West In History

Appendix 1
Other Historic Structures

In this appendix we list some two dozen buildings that reflect on the different periods of Key West in history. *None of these structures (with the exception of one converted to a shopping mall) are open to visitors for touring, and thus they should only be viewed from outside the property, from the street or sidewalk.* Due to tropical planting, flourishing palms, narrow streets, and modern automobile traffic and parking, many are difficult or impossible to photograph well, but one can still observe interesting architectural and historical details.

Wrecker Era 1820–1860

WILLIAM URIAH SAUNDERS HOUSE, 709 Eaton St. Saunders brought Bahamian influences to the design of this 1853 home.

JOHN BARTLUM HOUSE also known as "The Bahama House," 730 Eaton St. This home was actually built on Green Turtle Cay in the Bahamas in the early 1800s, then was moved by barge to Key West in 1847. Bartlum was a shipbuilder, known for building the first (and only) clipper ship ever constructed in Florida, the *Stephen R. Mallory.* The house had very low ceilings, more characteristic of homes in the Bahamas than those in Florida.

RICHARD ROBERTS HOUSE, 408 William St. Built in the Bahamas by Richard "Tuggy" Roberts, the brother-in-law of John Bartlum, this building was also moved to Key West in 1847.

GIDEON LOWE HOUSE, 409 William St. The rear portion of this home was originally built in the 1840s, later expanded in the 1870s.

BENJAMIN CURRY HOUSE, 610 Southard St. The house was built in 1856 by another Bahamian.

Civil War 1861–1865

COAST GUARD BUILDING/Clinton Square Market, Front St. Built in 1856 for coal storage for the navy, the structure was headquarters of the East Coast Blockade Squadron. The building was the naval administration headquarters until 1932, then coast guard offices into the 1970s. The structure is now a shopping mall and open to the public.

Age of Enterprise 1860s–1900

JOHN LOWE, JR. HOUSE, 620 Southard St. Finished in 1865, this was the family home of Lowe, a well-known wrecker who once worked as a clerk with the firm of William Curry. The house has had many functions, including a period in World War II as a USO canteen, and later, a hospital. The building features 12-foot ceilings and very few rooms off the central hall. Fairly rare in Key West, the building also has a widow's walk, actually used as a lookout point to spot ships wrecked ashore.

WARREN HOUSE/Old Town Manor, 511 Eaton St. Built in 1886 by Sam Otis Johnson. Johnson operated a general store next to the home, which was later moved to the rear of the house as a garage. The home was owned by Dr. Richard William Warren and family until the early 1970s.

THE PATTERSON HOUSE, 522 Caroline St. George B. Patterson built the home before 1889. He held a number of state and local government jobs, including judge of the district circuit court and city postmaster. The large Queen Anne structure features spindle-work friezes reflective of the Eastlake style of furniture, with turned pillars at the false second-floor balconies.

OTTO HOUSE/"The Artist House," 534 Eaton St. Thomas Osgood Otto built this Victorian home in the 1890s. Later it served as the residence of artist Eugene Otto. Eugene had owned "Robert, the haunted doll," as a child, whose story is now told in the East Martello Tower Museum. Eugene reportedly used the distinctive corner tower room of the Otto House as a studio.

PETER A. WILLIAMS HOUSE/"Donkey Milk House," 613 Eaton St. Built in 1866, the house gets its nickname because it backs onto Donkey Milk Alley, where late nineteenth century milkmen delivered not donkey milk but regular bottled cow milk from donkey-pulled carts.

FILER HOUSE, 724 Eaton St. Built in 1885, the house combines Victorian and Bahamian features. As a lumber merchant, Filer added many special gingerbread trimmings and a fancy etched transom at the front door.

ISLAND CITY HOUSE, 411 William St. This is another late 1800s private home for a wealthy merchant family. The building was transformed into a hotel when Flagler's railway to Key West opened in 1912. After the building fell into disrepair, it was condemned by the city. A major restoration in the 1970s rescued the structure.

WILLIAM RUSSELL HOUSE/Key West Bed and Breakfast, 415 William St. A home from about 1900, this building features ornamented columns on the front porch.

THE ROBERTS HOMES, 512 & 516 William St. Number 512, built in the 1890s by Charles Roberts, features "eyebrows," a local genre item of upper windows shaded by roofs. Charles' brother, John Samuel Roberts, built number 516 at the same time. Both feature Victorian gingerbread.

EDWARDS ROBERTS HOUSE, 643 William St. This building is also an eyebrow home from the late nineteenth century. Edwards Roberts was both a shipbuilder and stonemason.

BENJAMIN BAKER HOUSE, or "The Gingerbread House," 615 Elizabeth St. This home was built by businessman Baker in 1872 as a wedding gift for his daughter. It is highly decorated with Victorian gingerbread trim. However, as noted by architectural historian Alex Caemmerer, the house has very few other features of the Victorian style, lacking towers, balconies, or added false porches; Caemmerer classifies the home as "folk Victorian."

JOHN HASKINS BUILDING/Marquesa Hotel, Simonton and Fleming Sts. Constructed in 1884, and escaping destruction by the 1886 fire, the structure has seen a succession of businesses: haberdashery, drugstore, headquarters for the gas company, a car dealership, and a grocery. In the 1980s the building was entirely remodeled to host the modern hotel and restaurant.

DANE ALLEY/Simonton Court, 320 Simonton St. A cigar factory in the late 1800s, one can still find the former cigar-makers cottages behind the main building. The historic structures now host tourists.

CLAUDE ROBERTS HOUSE/ Bagatelle, 115 Duval St. Built for a foreman at the Cortez Cigar Factory, the home was originally on Fleming Street. The building was moved down Duval Street to the present spot in the 1970, during expansion of the Monroe County Library.

WILLIAM R. KERR HOUSE, 410 Simonton St. Architect Kerr designed this home for himself about 1880, featuring "carpenter gothic" elements. Kerr designed several commercial buildings around Key West, including the Old Post Office and Customs House, in the Richardsonian Romanesque style.

RICHARD KEMP HOUSE/Cypress House, Simonton and Caroline Sts. This home, built by prosperous sponge merchants, reflected Bahamian styles. It was built after the 1886 fire. The original pine and cypress could go unpainted due to natural resistance to weather and insects.

GEORGE BARTLUM HOUSE, 531 Caroline St. Bartlum, another successful sponge trader, finished this New England type home in 1888. Florida State Senator John Spottswood and his wife Mary lived there In the 1940s and President Truman and his wife Bess Truman often visited the Spottswoods in this home.

Twentieth Century

WINDSOR VILLAGE/Writer's Compound, 713–727 Windsor Lane. In this compound, several small original plots are joined together, with a combination of restoration and new construction. This fairly old compound, dating back to the 1950s, once hosted writers John Hersey, John Ciardi, Richard Wilbur, and Ralph Ellison, giving it the name "The Writer's Compound."

Appendix 2
Chronology: Key West in History

1513 Ponce de Leon discovers the Florida Keys and calls them the "Martyrs."

1500s-1820 The Spanish refer to Key West as Cayo Hueso—"Bone Key." There is no permanent settlement on Key West—fishermen and temporary wrecker camps only.

1622 The Spanish treasure ship *Nuestra Señora de Atocha* sinks in storm 35 miles west of Key West.

1763-1783 Florida is ceded to Britain after the "Seven Years War" and remains under British control for twenty years.

1783 Florida is returned to Spanish control at the end of the American War of Independence (American Revolution).

1815 Juan Pablo Salas gets title to Key West from Spanish government.

1819 Salas sells Key West to John Simonton; holdings are divided among Simonton, John Fleeming, John Whitehead, and Pardon C. Greene.

1821 The United States acquires Florida from Spain in Adams-Onis Treaty.

1822 Commodore David Porter establishes the Navy base at Key West; he calls Key West "Thompson Island" after Secretary of the Navy.

1825 The claims to Key West of pioneers Whitehead, Fleeming, Greene, and Simonton are confirmed by court.

1823-25 Commodore David Porter operates the "Mosquito Fleet" to suppress Caribbean pirates, with small boats named for insects.

1824 Fajardo Incident: U.S. troops under Lt. Charles Platt land in Puerto Rico and are arrested by Spanish authorities, leading to Commodore Porter's court martial and resignation from U.S. Navy.

1825 The first lighthouse in Key West is built.

1825-27 Three more lighthouses are set up on the Keys.

1828 The Wrecker Court is established in Key West under Judge James Webb.

1832 John James Audubon visits Key West; he paints white-crowned pigeon.

1839 Judge William Marvin takes over Wrecker Court and serves until 1863.

1838 William Whitehead completes sketch of view from Tift warehouse.

1845 William Curry enters the wrecking business, becoming one of richest men in Florida.

1845 Fort Zachary Taylor construction begins; it is completed in 1866.

1846 The first recorded Catholic mass is held in Key West.

1846 A severe hurricane strikes Key West, killing about 40 persons.

1851 First Catholic church in Key West is built.

1851 Asa Tift builds mansion on Whitehead Street, later to become the residence of Ernest Hemingway.

1855 William Curry begins construction of mansion, now Curry Mansion Inn.

1856 The Isaac Allerton sinks near Saddlebunch Key.

1860 The U.S. Navy brings seized slave ships to Key West; fatalities are buried at Higgs Beach.

1861 Florida secedes from the Union.

1861 The Civil War begins; U.S. troops at Fort Zachary Taylor and Navy personnel hold Key West for the Union.

1861 Stephen Mallory, Key West maritime attorney, departs for Richmond to become secretary of the navy for the Confederacy.

1861 The U.S.S. *San Jacinto,* on way to Key West, stops H.M.S. *Trent,* causing major U.S.-British international incident. Bell from *San Jacinto* is now on display at Customs House Museum.

1861-62 Key West wrecker and entrepreneur Asa Tift goes to New Orleans to build the warship Mississippi for the Confederacy.

1862 Admiral David Dixon Porter leads gunboat flotilla from Key West to assist in capture of New Orleans from Confederates.

1862-65 U.S. Navy blockading squadrons operate from Key West to help enforce blockade of the Confederacy.

1863-4 Two Martello Towers are built in Key West.

1865 Abraham Lincoln is assassinated, eight accused co-conspirators of John Wilkes Booth tried, and four are executed.

1865 Civil War ends.

1865 60 Four convicted Lincoln assassination co-conspirators, including Dr. Samuel Mudd, are sent to confinement at Fort Jefferson.

1865 Judge William Marvin of Key West briefly serves as Florida governor.

1866 A Civil War Memorial (Union) is erected across from the Customs House.

1867 The first overseas cable from U.S. to Cuba is installed in Key West at Southernmost Point.

1868-1878 The Ten Years War is fought in Cuba; rebels are defeated.

1860s-1910s Pineapples raised in Keys are shipped via Key West until supplanted by foreign imports.

1874 Eduardo Gato opens a cigar factory in Key West; the local cigar business expands over next twenty years.

1879 The Wall Warehouse is built.

1879 The "Guerra Chica" (Little War) rebellion is fought in Cuba.

1883 José Martí delivers speech at La Terraza de Martí in Key West.

1885 The Peacon ("Octagon") House is built.

1886 Fire sweeps Key West.

1887 to 1900 The sponge business thrives in Key West; it is supplanted at the beginning of the twentieth century by divers using diving suits out of Tarpon Springs, Florida.

1890 Armand Granday sets up a turtle soup business in Key West.

1891 Florida First National Bank, on the corner Duval and Front Streets, is constructed in Neo Mudéjar style.

1893 William Curry son-in-law, Martin Hellings, builds a mansion at 319 Duval Street, later Key West Woman's Club.

1895 José Martí is killed during the rebellion against Spanish rule in Cuba.

1896 Southernmost House is built by William Curry's son-in-law Jeptha Vining Harris.

1898 U.S.S. *Maine* explodes in Havana harbor; Spanish-American War is fought; Cuba gains independence.

1901 First Catholic Star of the Sea church is destroyed in storm.

1904 The Basilica of Mary Star of the Sea is built.

1905 Construction begins on the Over-Sea Railroad from Miami to Key West.

1911 Eduardo Gato turns his home over for use as a hospital for the poor.

1912 Henry Flagler opens the Over-Sea Railroad.

1917 Present-day cable hut at Southernmost Point is completed.

1919-20 Instituto de San Carlos is rebuilt at 516 Duval Street.

1920-1933 Prohibition is in effect in the United States, banning the sale of alcoholic beverages, but not their consumption; rum runners operate from Cuba to Key West.

1924 A Civil War Monument (Confederate) is erected in Bayview Park.

1928 Ernest Hemingway first visits Key West; staying at Casa Antigua, he works on his World War I novel, *A Farewell to Arms*.

1932-1939 Hemingway, living at former home of Asa Tift at 907 Whitehead Street, writes these books: *Death in the Afternoon, Green Hills of Africa, To Have and Have Not, The Snows of Kilamanjaro,* and *For Whom the Bell Tolls*.

1933 Sloppy Joe's bar relocates from prior site at 428 Greene Street, now Tony's Saloon.

1935 Hurricane destroys Over-Sea Railroad link from Miami to Key West.

1934-38 Julius Stone Jr., New Deal federal emergency relief administrator, helps fund Key West art colony, reduce unemployment, and begin restoration of the town.

1938 Key West Aquarium is built and opened with New Deal federal assistance.

1941-1945 World War II. Anti-submarine air and sea patrols and convoys operate out of Key West.

1941-1945 U.S. Coast Guard cutter *Ingham* serves on convoy patrols; the ship is now on exhibit in Key West.

1946-1952 President Harry S. Truman visits Key West at the Little White House.

1950 New shrimp fishing areas are discovered off Key West, beginning the period of flourishing shrimp fleet.

1955 The Margaret-Truman Launderette is opened.

1960 The Key West Art Center reopens.

1962 The Cuban Missile Crisis takes place; HAWK missile sites are set up in Key West.

1969 The Key West Lighthouse is decommissioned.

1977 Jimmy Buffett records "Margaritaville," celebrating Key West life-style.

1980 The Mariel Boatlift brings thousands of Cuban refugees through Key West.

1982 The "Conch Republic" is established.

1983 The "Southernmost Point Buoy" is set up.

1985 Mel Fisher recovers wreckage of the *Atocha*.

1987 Mel Fisher purchases building for Maritime Museum.

1997 The Key West AIDS Memorial is dedicated to local victims of the disease.

2003 The Key West Nature and Butterfly Conservatory opens.

2003 The Key West War Memorial in Mallory Square is dedicated.

Bibliography

There are numerous guidebooks to Key West, as well as a host of fictional works set in Key West. For this work, we drew material from visits to the sites, discussions with local docents, curators, proprietors, and hosts, information from historic markers, plaques, brochures, and the local history website: *www.keywesthistoricmarkertour.org.* Where information was inconsistent, we relied on the best-documented source.

In particular, we drew on the following works for specific aspects of the story of Key West in history, and we recommend this short list as especially informative.

Browne, Jefferson B. *Key West, the Old and the New.* The Record Company, 1912. Available on line at https://archive.org/details/keywestoldnew00brow

Burke, J. Wills. *The Streets of Key West. A History through Street Names.* Pineapple Press, 2014.

Caemmerer, Alex. *The Houses of Key West.* Pineapple Press, 1992.

Garnett, Burt, "Rum-running in the Economy of the Keys." *Martello,* 1967 Vol. 4, at http://www.speakeasyinn.com/history.htm

McIver, Stuart. *Hemingway's Key West.* Pineapple Press, 2013.

Rieser, Alison. *The Case of the Green Turtle: An Uncensored History of a Conservation Icon.* Johns Hopkins University Press, 2012.

Scandula, Jani. *Down in the Dumps: Place, Modernity, American Depression.* Duke University Press, 2008. (Chapter on Key West)

Standford, Les. *Last Train to Paradise: Henry Flagler and the Spectacular Rise and Fall of the Railroad That Crossed an Ocean.* Broadway Books, 2008.

Wolz, Robert, *The Legacy of the Harry S. Truman Little White House Key West.* Historic Tours of America, 2004.

Index

Notes: An entry that includes "(private)" indicates the building is privately owned and not open to touring; it may be viewed from the street side only. Ship names are shown in italics, e.g., *Atocha.*

Here are some other books from Pineapple Press on related topics. For a complete catalog, write to Pineapple Press, P.O. Box 3889, Sarasota, Florida, 34230-3889, or call (800) 746-5275. Or visit our website at www.pineapplepress.com.

St. Augustine in History by Rodney and Loretta Carlisle. Over 70 sites in historical context, era by era.

Grits & Grunts: Folkloric Key West by Stetson Kennedy. A portrait of Key West in the first half of the 20th century. A treasure trove of the rich multi-culture of the time by one of America's pre-eminent folklorists. Also an abundant sampling of the Key West art of Mario Sanchez.

Hemingway's Key West by Stuart McIver. A vivid portrait of the legendary writer's life in Key West. A tour of his favorite Key West and Havana haunts.

Over Key West and the Florida Keys by Charles Feil. A gorgeous album featuring aerial photographs of islands large and small, glistening waters, and serene communities. Captions provide bits of Keys history.

The Florida Keys by John Viele. The trials and successes of the Keys pioneers are brought to life in this series, which recounts tales of early pioneer life and life at sea. **Volume 1:** *A History of the Pioneers;* **Volume 2:** *True Stories of the Perilous Straits;* **Volume 3:** *The Wreckers.*

Florida Keys Impressions by Millard Wells. A famed watercolorist offers his unique impression of the Keys, with their blend of cultures, vegetation, architecture, birds, water, boats—all with that laid-back attitude.

The Streets of Key West: A History Through Street Names by J. Wills Burke. Simonton, Duval, Whitehead, Truman: discover how these and other Key West streets came by their names.

Mario Sanchez: Better Than Ever, a collection and commentary by Nance Frank. 54 color reproductions of work by the famed Key West artist Mario Sanchez (1908-2005).

The Houses of Key West by Alex Caemmerer. Explore the architectural treasure trove of Key West's 19th century houses.

Hemingway's Cats: An Illustrated Biography by Carlene Fredericka Brennen. Explores the life of Ernest Hemingway, the women he loved, and the cats and dogs he befriended throughout his life. Filled with photographs, many never before published.

Florida's Great Ocean Railway by Dan Gallagher. The incredible story of the building of the Key West Extension on the Florida East Coast Railway from Miami to Key West from 1905 to 1916.

Florida's Past Volumes 1, 2, and 3 by Gene Burnett. Collected essays from Burnett's "Florida's Past" columns in *Florida Trend* magazine, plus some original writings not found elsewhere. Burnett's easygoing style and his sometimes surprising choice of topics make history good reading.

Key Biscayne by Joan Gill Blank. This engaging history of the southernmost barrier island in the U.S. tells the stories of its owners and would-be owners.

Southeast Florida Pioneers by William McGoun. Meet the pioneers of the Palm Beach area, the Treasure Coast, and Lake Okeechobee in this collection of well told, fact-filled stories from the 1690s to the 1990s.